breath prayer

christine
valters paintner

breath prayer

an ancient practice for the
EVERYDAY SACRED

BROADLEAF BOOKS
MINNEAPOLIS

A new moon teaches gradualness
and deliberation, and how one gives birth
to oneself slowly. Patience with small details
makes perfect a large work, like the universe.
What nine months of attention does for an embryo
forty early mornings alone will do
for your gradually growing wholeness.

—Rumi

contents

introduction

The Divine has sent us a Comforter
in the form of our own breath.
Press out her healing nectar.
What flows so naturally can only be good.

Nothing is gained by listening to the voices of fear
that others have placed in your mind.
Listen instead to the music of So'ham
pouring through your flesh.

Inhalation is wine. Exhalation is surrender.
Beauty does not stream down from above.
It murmurs from the well of Silence in your heart.
Silence is the Mother. You are her song.

—Alfred K. LaMotte

Many religious traditions have some version of breath prayer. In my own tradition, the roots of breath prayer are built from St. Paul's invitation to people who hold faith to "pray without ceasing." In early Christianity, many monks and nuns would endeavor to do exactly this in practice by bringing prayer to each breath. They would combine a phrase of prayer or blessing with the inhale and exhale so that every breath was a chance for them to be present to the sacred. In earliest tradition, the words they used were

Lord Jesus Christ, Son of God (inhale)
have mercy on me a sinner (exhale)

—known as the Jesus Prayer or the Prayer of the Heart. This prayer and prayer form originated in the sixth century, but the text is taken from words spoken to Jesus, as recorded in the gospels, in the first century.

This kind of "mantra" practice has also long been present in the Hindu tradition, where a sacred phrase is repeated as an anchor to keep one's awareness focused on the divine at work in the world. In the Buddhist tradition, these take the form of *gathas*, short verses recited with the breath, as part of mindfulness practice and meditation, and recited during ordinary activities, like walking, working, or cleaning and so on.

In Sufism it is the *dhikr* prayer that is repeated to help in remembering the sacred presence. Jews pray the Shema, "Hear O Israel: the Lord our God, the Lord is One," recited as part of morning and evening prayers and also before sleeping. Some consider it to be the most important prayer they offer. Some Christians pray with the rosary, which is a prescribed set of prayers to repeat again and again while using beads to mark your way. While some who pray the Shema or the rosary don't always equate the prayer form with breath, for those who observe the way the prayer is embodied, repeated, they witness the breath and cadence so close in form that for many it is considered a form of breath prayer.

Give Me a Word

In ancient times, wise men and women fled out into the desert of what is now the Middle East and Northern Africa. There, they found a place so stripped barren and wild they could be fully present to the divine and to their own inner struggles. To them, the desert became a place to enter into silence, the refiner's fire, and be stripped down to one's holy essence. The desert was a threshold place where, they believed, you emerged different from when you entered.

4

As people heard about the wisdom of those entering the desert, many followed these *ammas* and *abbas*, seeking them out, asking them for wisdom and guidance for a meaningful life. One tradition of seekers was to ask the wise ones of the desert for "a word"—a word or phrase on which to ponder for many days, weeks, months, or sometimes a whole lifetime. This practice came to be connected to *lectio divina*, where we approach a sacred text with the same request: "Give me a word." We ask to meet something in the text that will nourish us, challenge us, a word or phrase or line we can wrestle with and grow into. The word that is given has the potential to transform us.

Whatever your spiritual or religious background might be, this book is meant to provide an invitation for us to practice this seeking of a life-giving "word" to help direct our attention in various moments of the day toward what is most sacred.

To reflect both the desert tradition and also the different religious traditions, I have chosen to begin with the many ordinary practices such as showering, cooking, and driving, and written a short breath prayer—or what's sometimes called a poem prayer—to accompany it. These are prayers you might learn by heart and recite gently to yourself as you perform the task, as a way of bringing a meditative awareness to all you do. If you are familiar with the practice of centering prayer, it is similar to repeating the word or phrase as an anchor for your attention, but in all the activities of daily life. In also seeking to bring that aspect of "a word" that might change us, I've also sought to focus on words or phrases that, combined with breath, might transform us as we engage and breathe them, over days and weeks and even a lifetime.

Breath by Breath

In the *Philokalia*, the great collection of Eastern Christian wisdom books, which also teaches about the early practice of the Jesus Prayer, St. Hesychios the Priest writes, "Let the name of Jesus adhere to your breath, and then you will know the blessings of stillness." I love this image of letting the prayer adhere to your breath. Rather than a forcing together of word and breath, imagine the words naturally being drawn to the breath like a magnet to metal or like bees to flowers. In this bringing together, the "blessings of stillness" wash over you.

Our breath is such an intimate companion. One that sustains us moment by moment even as we are entirely unaware of that sustaining gift. Yet when we bring our intention to it, it also becomes an ally for slowing down, for touching stillness.

These prayers are meant to be gateways—both to bring you more present to the sacredness of whatever activity you are involved in, and also, perhaps, to your own practice of writing short phrases for prayer to learn by heart. I'll offer guidance for your own creation of that paired praying practice at the end of the book.

The intention and focus throughout the book is not on saying each prayer correctly or perfectly each time, but on letting the words open your heart to a deeper intention in daily living. We work on the words, but the words work on us as well. Eventually, you might discover that you are not so much reciting the prayer as the prayer is reciting you, guiding you, opening your heart to a devotion to the world.

Learning by Heart

When we memorize something, like a prayer or line from a poem, we often describe it as "learning by heart." Many of the early Christian monastics would have learned large quantities of Scripture—especially the psalms, which made up the cycle of their daily prayer—by heart, largely out of necessity because of the scarcity and expense of books. The practice of *lectio divina*, or sacred reading, was meant to be a deep listening of the heart to words and phrases

7

of the psalms or sacred texts. That deep listening practice was likened to a cow chewing her cud, the slow process of breaking something down, digesting it, and allowing it to nourish us.

In the Hebrew Scriptures we find many passages that describe the new covenant as not written on stone, but in the hearts of the people. This was meant to indicate a shift from following an external list of rules to a true internal experience of conversion. The motivation to do good things—to live from the wisdom of the heart and to bring that active good into the world—comes from an internal motivation (the heart) rather than an external one (rules).

Many of us might have experienced at school the assignment to memorize certain material, whether the periodic table of elements or lines for a play. For most of us, it wasn't often done as a way to cultivate a love for something, or as a process of conversion or transformation, but more as a practical endeavor. Unless we have a true heart connection to what we're memorizing "by heart," we aren't likely to see the value in what we are doing. But perhaps there have been things you have memorized in the past that you are grateful to have in your heart, whether lines from Scripture or a poem, or even words from a conversation with a friend that impacted you in some way. These all have the potential to bring about our transformation.

In an age of digital access when we are so accustomed to having the texts at hand, I wonder what it would be like if those words didn't live on paper or digitally, but were inscribed on our hearts. How might we be shaped by their invitation in new ways?

I am not very good at memorizing things. I tend to be a big-picture person rather than one for small details. But I also know the tremendous gift it has been for me to be able to recall a line from a poem that speaks to the moment I am in. Words that are already inscribed in my heart seem to arise just when they are most needed.

As you consider learning these breath prayers, you might want to bring the written text of the prayer on a walk with you. Recite the words as you walk, letting them fall into the rhythm of your steps and become embodied. If you stumble on a line, simply look at the paper and find your way again. When we learn by heart while walking, we are embodying the rhythm of the words into our muscles and bones as well as our breath.

Writing This Book

There were several threads that came together in the writing of this book. First came the invitation from an editor I had worked with years ago. She suggested I read Thich

Nhat Hanh's book *Present Moment, Wonderful Moment: Mindfulness Verses for Daily Living* in which he introduces the Buddhist practice of gathas, short prayers to be said in rhythm with the breath while engaging in ordinary tasks. She wondered if the concept might inspire my own book. And I found a doorway into exploring the Jesus Prayer in Christianity. These were the first seeds for the book you are now holding.

In March of 2020 the pandemic hit the world, and Ireland where I live, like many other places, went into full lockdown for close to three months. We were only allowed to travel a maximum of two kilometers for exercise. As someone with a strong hermit side who also loves time at home, this kind of compassionate retreating came naturally. My husband and I both welcomed the greater solitude even as we shared the grief of so many around the world struggling in this time.

As things began to open up and we were allowed to travel further from home, I realized I had discovered a hidden gift through this experience. I came to fall even more in love with the most ordinary moments of my days. All the tasks and activities that sustain me became infused with a sense of wonder. Writing this book during those months assisted this grace breaking open as I felt enormous gratitude for this particular project at this moment of my life. I savored the way this practice of breath prayer brought me into intimate encounter with all of the mundane but marvelous aspects of my life.

The more I read about breath prayer, the more I discovered that forms of this practice are at the heart of many traditions, even the practice of saying blessings for all the ordinary moments and activities of the day found in both Jewish and Celtic traditions. These spiritualities all encourage seekers to slow down, pause, and bring a deep reverence for the most ordinary tasks of life and moments of the day. Most traditions have prayers like this to remind us of what is sacred, to help us to cherish life as itself an embodied prayer.

Monastic Influence

In my own work, the three main streams of Christian spiritual tradition that call to me are the wisdom of the desert mothers and fathers, Celtic monasticism, and Benedictine spirituality. And there, too, I have rediscovered this prayer practice, as the Celtic and Benedictine paths were both deeply influenced by the stories passed down from the desert wisdom keepers as well as the spirituality of the Eastern Orthodox church, where the Jesus Prayer has its origins.

I have come to see this rich contemplative way as a path of nonlinear, nondualistic, nondirected, intuitive consciousness. These are qualities that we might describe as "feminine," in contrast to more linear, productivity-oriented, rational ways of thinking. We need both, of course, and we each contain the possibility to hold both within us, whatever our gender. When we embrace this other mode of being in the world, we bring great gifts that aren't possible any other way.

This, for me, is perhaps the greatest gift of monastic practice and its careful guidance to the heart of stillness—to immerse us in a way of being and perceiving the world that moves us past finding value solely in our doing. When we discover the immense riches in our very being, we can rest our concerted efforts to get ahead, to achieve something, to produce. Because these have become the primary motivators of our human culture, the shadow aspects of them have meant that we exploit and destroy nature to fulfill these goals.

The ancient writers of the *Philokalia*, an Eastern Orthodox Christian text teaching the heart of contemplation, wrote with great love about this pathway to the place of inner refuge and sanctuary. It is only through our own willingness to embrace a radical humility and vulnerability that we can soften enough to allow the grace that is there to penetrate our daily awareness. It is only by entering into the unknowing of the heart that we are illuminated by its mysteries. Praying with the breath was

12

a key way to do this; each inhale and exhale becomes a portal to divine presence and inner stillness.

Our senses ground us and orient us in the world *and* to a world behind this world. This is the truth that any mystical tradition seeks to convey. It is not that the earthly realm is to be ignored or transcended, but when we taste what is most real, what endures, then everything our senses perceive in the world is infused with a radiance. Again, we are not called to choose between physical or spiritual but rather to see them as magnificently woven together; we can see beneath the surface of things as our senses become the gateway to a deeper layer everywhere we look. Ordinary tasks become luminous with grace.

Ultimately our contemplative practice leads us into deeper love with the world and into compassionate action on behalf of other beings. This is how we know we are having a genuine encounter with the holy—it leads us away from the illusion of separateness and toward a deeper care for humanity and creation. The contemplative vision sees that we are all bound together in a communion of love.

Practicing Presence

These breath prayers help us to cultivate some essential skills for our spiritual lives. The first of these is presence.

For the desert mothers and fathers, sitting in their cell and staying present to the moment was the whole of their practice. In one story, Abba John gave this advice: "Watching means to sit in the cell and be always mindful of God. This is what is meant by, 'I was on watch and God came to me' (Matt 25:36)."

The Greek word *nepsis* means "watchfulness." It refers to a kind of calm vigilance in daily life, staying attentive and aware to the inner movements of the heart, watching one's thoughts, and noticing the patterns that arise. This inner attention, conducted with compassion, is the grace of the desert way. Practicing presence and paying attention is a skill we can also develop. It means holding the moment lightly, not obsessing over it or being disturbed by it, but staying calm and attentive.

Whatever experience we are engaged in, whatever challenge we face, becomes our monastic cell, the place where we can watch and encounter the divine presence in our midst. The desert fathers and mothers invite us to practice this kind of interior watchfulness where we witness what happens inside our minds and hearts with compassion and commitment.

They knew that watchfulness is the antithesis of numbing ourselves to life, whether through binge-watching hours of television, feeding our anxiety through news cycle addictions, losing ourselves on the internet, shopping, eating, drinking—or whatever numbs us from ourselves and from an awareness of the needs of others. Anything can serve as a way of numbing ourselves when we engage in it as a way of avoiding what we are experiencing within.

Practicing Stability

Connected to presence is the willingness to stay with our experience. The desert elders counselled to "sit in your cell and your cell will teach you everything." The Indian poet Kabir wrote, "I felt in need of a great pilgrimage so sat still for three days and God came to me." In the Benedictine tradition, monastics commit themselves to stability, which, on one level, means never leaving the monastic order they have vowed to stay in. On another level, it is about not running away as soon as boredom sets in or conflict arises. We all have ways to distract or numb ourselves and escape this moment we find ourselves in. Stability is about bringing ourselves fully to this present moment and staying in it. Stay in that inner cell that offers up its wisdom when we allow ourselves to sustain our attention that long.

We live in such a rushed culture that even those of us committed to contemplative rhythms may find ourselves unnaturally hurrying to get on to the next thing or deadline. When committing to stability, I also see how often

15

I don't allow myself time to just linger between things. There are holy pauses in the moments between things. In monastic tradition, the practice of *statio* is an invitation to linger in these thresholds a while before rushing on to the next thing.

Breath prayers are a way to help me slow down and savor my experience, to pause and reflect on what I have encountered, to anticipate what I will commit myself to doing next. In the heart of whatever thing I am doing, whether working or showering or eating, I can find a sanctuary space in each moment that allows me to also cultivate my capacity for just being, bringing that gift to each time of doing so there is more restfulness in each activity. I can yield my need to be productive and offer up my practice to the Holy One. We can extend this even further beyond the daily tasks of life to our work in the world. Breath prayers help to sustain us by offering a deep well of nourishment we can drink from in the midst of our activities. They help to replenish us for the real and necessary work of being a healing presence in the world with our neighbors and communities.

Practicing Gratitude

Finally, these breath prayers are, at heart, about practicing full presence to what we are doing in the moment and feeling a sense of gratitude for the gift of the experience.

The fifth-century monk and mystic Benedict of Nursia counsels in his Rule for monastic life an attitude of contentment among his community. Whatever circumstances they are in, they are to find some satisfaction with what is in the moment. In a world of self-entitlement and inflated sense of need, learning to be content with what we have has the potential to be revolutionary. It means craving less and being more satisfied with what one has.

One way to encourage this posture of contentment in our lives is to practice gratitude. Gratitude is a way of being in the world that does not assume we are owed anything, and the fact that we have something at all, whether our lives, our breath, families, friends, shelter, laughter, or other simple pleasures, is cause for celebration. We can cultivate a way of being in the world that treats all these things as gifts, knowing none of us "deserves" particular graces.

We might begin each day simply with an expression of gratitude for the most basic of gifts, life itself. Awakening each morning for another day to live and love, grateful for our breath and a body that allows us to move through our day. Then we can offer gratitude for a home and all the things that are important to us about this place of shelter. There are many breath prayers in this collection that help us with this stance toward our lives.

Gratitude is a practice that can begin with the smallest acknowledgment and be expanded out to every facet of our existence. A very simple way to nurture this awareness in our lives is to end each day with five minutes of slow breathing and just saying *thank* on the in-breath and *you* on the out-breath. While breathing and expressing thanks, simply let the day unfold in your imagination and notice what your heart feels drawn toward. See what large and small moments of grace want to be lifted up. It is a way to end the day by honoring the gifts we have received rather than dwelling on where life came up short for us.

Gratitude has a way of transforming our approach to life into one that is more open-hearted, generous, and joyful. Rather than moving through our day feeling cynical or burdened, we can consciously choose our thoughts, attend to the breath. We might then be able to tap into greater joy to replenish us for those moments when we do need to fight for dignity and kindness. Gratitude makes us feel connected to something bigger than ourselves.

Journeying through These Pages

This book can be read front to back or simply as an invitation to see what speaks to you. You might scroll through the topics in the table of contents and see if there is a particular activity that calls to you. It could be that you want to be more aware while eating, or perhaps you find your phone a source of continual distraction and disconnection and that chapter invites you to pay attention differently. See if one of the suggestions below "shimmers" for you or calls your attention in some way.

The prayers are short and designed to be retained, remembered, learned by heart. Commit to reciting each one to yourself during that activity for a few days. Notice the quality of your awareness. Slowly add in other prayers to your day, over time. Eventually, you might create your own prayers, which we'll explore at the end of this book.

The breath prayers encompass some activities where it perhaps feels easy to love what we are doing, like eating, walking, or sitting with a companion animal. They invite you to see the sacred when cleaning or sending a message to someone. And they also include more challenging moments like reading the news, waking in the middle of the night, sitting with grief, or feeling moments of anxiety around climate change and extinction.

This book begins with a quote from the Sufi poet Rumi about how forty early mornings will nourish your growing wholeness. Forty is considered a sacred number in many traditions. In the Hebrew Bible, there's a story of how the Israelites spent forty years in the wilderness. In Christian tradition, there's the story of Jesus spending forty days in the desert on retreat before starting his public ministry. The season of Lent is a set of forty days when we are invited to make a commitment to daily reflection.

In the tradition of reflection, habit building, and as Rumi puts it, nourishment, I have included forty breath prayers in this book. You might consider working through these prayers day by day, over a span of forty days. Or you can work with as many of the these forty as you feel inspired by. I hope you'll also turn to creating your own breath prayers, with ideas and guidance at the end of this book, for prayers you may be longing to express that haven't been included.

Also at the end of this book is a Notes section where you can dive more deeply into some of the works mentioned in this book and that inform my own breath practice.

You can choose forty days for your own personal retreat in everyday life, whether at Lent or during another season of your life when you want to practice slowing down and paying closer attention. Each day you can learn one of these prayers and practice it, or you can simply choose a few that speak to your heart and repeat them regularly. Notice how they move in you; maybe the prayers will develop as you repeat them and you will make them your own.

In the monastic practice of *lectio divina*, we read a text and listen for a word or phrase, let it unfold within us, and listen for a sense of invitation that arises from our engagement. In these practices, I am offering you the phrase to begin with, though with the invitation for you to choose which one most shimmers for you, and let that work in your heart for a period of time. Listen for the invitation that emerges from your practice.

As I mentioned, the closing chapter of this book is about creating your own breath prayers for all of the other tasks in life I didn't cover where you might want support in becoming more present.

Each breath prayer is short and rooted in presence and gratitude, created to support you in paying attention to the present moment, to whatever it is you are doing, or to rest more deeply into being. They are meant to help you celebrate some aspects of life's most ordinary beauty.

My deepest hope as you read this book is that you put into practice the wisdom it offers. It is, in some ways, an extraordinarily simple path, but not at all easy to follow. It demands discipline, showing up again and again. It requires a desire for that deep alignment with our truest nature, a willingness to release our defenses, and to rest in *hesychia*, or deep inner stillness the ancient orthodox writers described. The more we bathe in that space of silence, the more we might encounter the purest kind of joy and be transformed. Humility and practice are the seeds, but joy is the sweetest fruit.

entering the practice

I breathe in peace,
I breathe out love.

quieting myself to hear my heart

We begin just sitting quietly, savoring a few moments of stillness in our day. This might be first thing in the morning or at the end of day. Choose a time when you won't be interrupted for ten minutes.

This time of quiet is to simply practice aligning your prayer with your breathing. It gives time and space to become acquainted with this type of prayer. It offers the chance to slow down and discover the gifts that come when we cultivate an inner and outer silence and direct our attention to the Source of all peace and all love. This time of quiet prayer is the building block for the other prayers that follow. Once we become rooted in this rhythm of praying, we will be able to draw on it more naturally as we are engaged in our daily activities.

When we pray with the rhythm of the breath, it provides us an anchor in the midst of whatever we are doing. Breath is our constant companion, as is our heartbeat, and these gentle risings and fallings offer us the gift of a kind of scaffolding for our prayers.

The words simply give us direction for our attention. In the ancient traditions, often lines from Scripture or other traditional prayers were used. The words are less important than the intention behind them, but still, language can offer us imagery that guides our distracted minds toward a particular place. In the case of prayer, this place is the sacred presence beating in the heart of the world.

The prayers in this book were written to accompany the in-breath and out-breath. We begin with some very simple ones that make this obvious, such as this prayer below.

As you inhale, you whisper to yourself: *I breathe in peace*.

You might add an element of visualization to this as well. Perhaps images are a more potent form of prayer for you, in which case, as you breathe in, see yourself drawing in the gift of peace into your body. Notice what color or texture it is. Pay attention to your body's response as it fills you.

As you exhale, you say softly: *I breathe out love*.

Imagine inviting love to fill the world with each out-breath, see it filling every crack and corner. Again, notice any colors or textures. How does your body respond knowing love is being sent out to the world?

Sometimes words are the gateway to prayer for us, but sometimes words inspire visual or somatic responses, which are also part of the act of praying. Some of us are more verbal in our prayers, while some draw on the other senses to connect with the divine.

It is vital that we pause to pray in this way even when we don't feel like it. Perhaps our day has been especially not peaceful or loving. Maybe it felt filled with strife—conflict with loved ones or coworkers, or perhaps a sense of overwhelm at the suffering of the world, or maybe just a sense of unease and anxiety over so many unknowns. It is in these moments that we pause and remember the root of our root. We connect back to Source. We stop what we are doing to reconnect to the foundation of the world and of our lives. We act *as if* until we might experience just a small taste of the peace and love we seek.

It is especially important that we do not wait until we feel like it or are in the mood for this kind of prayer. Those moments may come but are often fleeting. We want to build the foundation of continual prayer into our days so that we might begin to see the possibility of loving attention at the heart of everything we do. We want to cultivate a way of seeing our lives that honors what happens when we slow down and pay attention.

As you sit and practice, you may find that your mind is distracted. You might breathe in peace and breathe out love for a few cycles and then find yourself thinking about the growing list of things to do, or feel concerned for a friend who is ill, or worry about whether your job is secure. The practice is to bring your attention back, again and again, to the breath, to the words, to the image of peace and love available to us and the world. We do this gently, knowing that distraction is an integral part of being human.

This is not a form of denial. It is a recognition. Distraction, worry, and anxiety will always be with us, and it can be helpful to intentionally set them aside for a few moments and allow ourselves to be filled with something else. While struggle is part of the truth of our human condition, grace, beauty, delight, and wonder are all part of that truth as well. We can choose where we focus our attention. We might discover that we return to the daily struggles with more resilience and clarity.

As you deepen into this practice of breathing and pairing words with the inhale and exhale, there is another kind of interruption that can happen. This is when you become so immersed in the prayer you discover the words and images are praying you, rather than you being the one to direct the prayer. In these moments, you may find yourself filled with a sense of deep and abiding love that breathes into you and out from you. It is also in these moments that you are hearing your heart.

The heart is the place of our deepest encounter with the divine in our lives. The Scriptures and ancient mystics describe the heart as the place of inner sanctuary where the spark of God lives within each of us. We always have this divine spark within us, but it can often be difficult to remember. Slowing down, becoming quiet, and paying attention to the breath opens gateways into this sanctuary space.

Once we have truly descended into the heart, we find ourselves less concerned with controlling the outcome of things and more open to following the sacred unfolding of our lives. We start to relax our incessant striving and grasping and discover a desire to yield ourselves, both body and soul, to a greater wisdom.

A Note about Breath Prayer and Medical Conditions

The purpose of these breath prayers is never to cause discomfort. We all have different rhythms of breath and lengths for our inhales and exhales that feel comfortable for us. I tried to create prayers where each line wasn't burdensomely long, either for the purposes of keeping the breath aligned or for memorization. However, if at any time you feel yourself straining to say a prayer and match it with your breath, please either change the words, shortening the length of the prayer, or change where the breaks are in the prayer so you pray fewer words with each inhale and exhale and the prayer spans more breath cycles.

31

You can choose to say these prayers aloud or silently in your heart. When said silently it may be easier to keep the suggested rhythm of inhale or exhale as you can speed up or slow down the words as needed. But as with any prayer form, this is meant to uplift your spirit, not become a physical challenge to meet.

Sophia (or Jesus, Mother, Father, Spirit)
be with me,
Sophia (or Jesus, Mother, Father, Spirit)
guide me

praying with the divine name

The Jesus prayer, which serves as one of the primary inspirations for these breath prayer practices, leans very deeply into saying the name of Jesus as the heart of the prayer. Repeating the name of Jesus itself becomes a place of encounter with the mystery of Christ.

In my own teaching and practice, I try to keep the names for the divine reality spacious and open ended. I am aware that any time I am teaching or leading a meditation, those who are listening may come from a wide spectrum of belief and imagery for the reality we sometimes name God. Some of the heavily masculine imagery like Lord can feel restrictive to some, while for others it may feel like coming home.

In the apophatic tradition of mysticism to which I'm deeply drawn, its ancient practitioners warn that getting too attached to a name for God was a distraction from the generous possibilities the divine being contains within itself. Anyone who has been through a "dark night of the soul" experience as described by Spanish mystic John of the Cross knows that it is only at the point of relinquishment of our images for the divine that God is then revealed in entirely new ways, ways that bring more spaciousness and possibility and honor the mystery.

You might experiment with this yourself as you read this book and see if adding a sacred name to the breath prayers helps to deepen the practice for you. Jesus, Spirit, Father, Mother, Holy Wisdom, Source, or one of many other possibilities could be added to any of the prayers contained here. If you do, I recommend you repeat the name twice—once on the in-breath and once on the out-breath before continuing with the prayer as it is written. You could also add a few words, as with the breath prayer below.

Quieting the heart, we simply rest into the divine name of the Holy One, however we feel most led and nourished.

You could simply pray:

Breathe in: *Sophia*
Breathe out: *Sophia*

Or you could add a few words that help direct you to their presence.

Breathe in: *Jesus, be with me*,
Breathe out: *Jesus, guide me*.

You can, of course, substitute any divine name here. This might be a breath prayer to repeat to yourself at any time of day when you want to feel that sacred connection and presence. You can also link this prayer with any of the other breath prayers offered in this book.

For example, with the first breath prayer introduced, I could add the divine name, like this:

Breathe in: *Spirit, be with me*,
Breathe out: *Spirit, guide me*.
Breathe in: *I breathe in peace*,
Breathe out: *I breathe out love*.

Let the divine name echo in the sanctuary of your heart, the place where the spark of God dwells within each of us. With each inhale, invite this sacred presence to be more fully with you. With each exhale, seek guidance from this divine indwelling. Imagine the sacred filling you with each inhale, noticing images as well as colors and body sensations that arise. With each exhale, notice how this presence wants to move in you and guide you through your day. As you let go of your need to direct the process, listen for the holy direction that is revealed.

In the prayers that follow, I intentionally leave specific divine names out to allow you the spaciousness to call upon God in the way you feel most inspired to. You can add the name that most resonates with you to each prayer, or you can just hold the awareness of leaning into the divine mystery as you utter the prayers that follow, without saying the name, but feeling your own longing and resting into that presence. Our intention can be a very powerful way to connect to the sacred.

I recommend you start the prayers that follow more simply at first, with the prayer as written. Then, as you develop this practice, notice the longings of your heart. See how you desire to pray and, if it feels nourishing, add a divine name to each breath.

I breathe in possibility,
I breathe out gratitude.

awakening

awn is one of the sacred hinges of the day, a thresh-old moment when we move from darkness to light, and that shift to light can become a portal to a new begin-ning. Each morning when we awaken, we might open to the possibilities it offers us and practice gratitude for another day on this tender earth—for birdsong, for a sky full of color—as if Earth herself is offering a liturgy of praise we are invited to join.

In the first chapter, we explored tying a prayer to our breathing at any time of pause during the day. This was a practice to set a foundation and begin learning this way of weaving words and breath together to set our hearts on the sacred presence in all moments. The second chapter introduced praying with a divine name and connecting it to our breath prayers.

Now your invitation is to take a similar breath prayer and practice it during the first few moments of your awak-ening, as a way to set your intention for the day to come.

If you normally set an alarm to awaken each day, con-sider setting it ten minutes earlier. When it rings, see if you can forgo checking your phone for messages and rest for a few moments in that threshold space between sleeping and full alertness. The mind fully awake is often ready to get on with the plans of the day. The invitation here is to dwell for a little while longer in that in-between space where dreams and rest can still inform your way of being present to the moment. You might even write this breath prayer on a little card or piece of paper and leave it by your bed so it is the first thing you see in the morning.

As you inhale, say *I breathe in possibility*. Be present to the newness of this day. Before the cynicism of reading the news and daily living burdens your heart, allow yourself to rest into this place of openness and possibilities that may lie ahead.

As you exhale, say *I breathe out gratitude*. Be present to the gift of this day. Before resentment or desire for what you do not have can enter in, spend a few moments in gratitude for the simple gifts of breath, life, shelter. Let thanks fill your heart for the simple gift of waking up when it could be otherwise.

Again, if imagery helps in your prayer, consider breathing in and imagining the light of a new dawn filling your being. This moment when the promise of light returning again echoes the energies of spring, and we are invited to see the world with new eyes. Notice how your body feels in response to this awareness of the new moment dawning.

As you breathe out, see the color of gratitude filling you and flowing outward into the world. You don't need to direct it, just let it move through you and out. Pay attention to your body's response to the grace of gratitude being released.

Across the world, different religious traditions honor this time of awakening with various prayers and devotions. To bring our devotion to this moment is to join with millions of others in a cascade of prayer in celebration of what goodness might emerge in the day ahead. You might feel yourself part of a human community that honors the rhythms of creation, opening to the awe and wonder that comes with the blank page.

Rest into this prayer for a few minutes. Notice any inclinations to reach for your phone or your mind beginning to make plans for the day. Gently return to this breathing in and breathing out. Return to the words, *I breathe in possibility, I breathe out gratitude*. Stay present to the experience of the prayer in your heart and your body. Imagine with each breath that you are physically resting into the words and their meaning. Imagine you are softening any places of holding and tension and allow possibility and gratitude to move through you as fully as you can.

You might also experiment with keeping your eyes closed at first while praying this breath prayer. Notice what you see in that space of darkness, knowing that the light outside is emerging.

Then pray again with your eyes open, but with a soft gaze, not yet focused in a hard stare or trying to gain information like when reading. Open your eyes to the waiting page of the day, the white canvas, the stone in which the sculpture of your life pulses and awaits its revelation. Give thanks for a thousand creative possibilities awaiting you.

As you continue to cultivate this way of praying, first in any open space or moment, then in these times of waking up each morning, begin to notice how the prayer spills into the rest of your day. Do you notice any shifts in your awareness, or presence to the day, when you allow time to pause and focus on meeting the divine right here and now? Perhaps not, perhaps the prayer time itself is enough of a respite and sanctuary space. But perhaps it also prepares you to taste that sanctuary at other moments of the day as well.

You might also discover that this way of praying imagery with your breath creates a felt response to your breathing, so that even when you aren't holding this kind of present awareness you might still experience your breath as a threshold, inviting you to be here and now more fully at various points in the day.

You might also begin to bring an awareness of how the in-breath is akin to this moment of awakening, of the dawning of another day. The poet Mary Oliver asks, "Listen, are you breathing just a little and calling it a life?" The inhalation can be an invitation to consider the fullness of our breathing and the fullness of our living.

Similarly, the out-breath is akin to evening and the arrival of dusk, when we become aware of the endings of things. The exhalation invites us to consider what we long to carry with us into the night and what we can release.

Each new inhalation throughout the day can help us remember the moment of first awakening and the experience of possibility and gratitude we allowed ourselves to dwell in.

the grace of daily tasks

Water and soap become sacrament,
each day a new baptism.

showering

I t is easy to take showering for granted; water seems to flow so easily into our homes, until we have trouble with our pipes or our water heater breaks down.

In many traditions, water is at the heart of a sacramental action, whether baptism or blessing in Christianity, the *mikvah* for purification in Judaism, or the sacredness of the River Ganges, which is considered to be the divine mother in Hinduism and is a site for daily rituals.

In the Hebrew Scriptures, the prophet Amos tells us justice will roll down like waters and righteousness like an ever-living stream. Our time in the shower is a perfect moment to commune with the gift of water, to give thanks for its presence in our lives, to pray for those without it, and to ask for a renewed perspective on the day ahead. Like the holy water fonts at the entrances to churches, showering is an opportunity to bless ourselves and express gratitude for its gift.

For this breath prayer, we continue to pray with the inhale and exhale, but I have not included the language of "I breathe in . . . I breathe out . . ." in the prayer itself this time. Know you can always add it back in if that feels helpful.

Step into the shower and feel the warmth of the water rushing over you. I know for myself, a shower helps to awaken me to the day and the warmth brings ease to any aching joints.

As you breathe in, say *Water and soap become sacrament*. You might pour some shampoo in your hand or lather up your bar of soap and become aware of how such simple things in life like water and soap can break us open to a much wider truth in the moment.

As you breathe out, say *each day a new baptism*. As you rinse yourself clean from dirt and soap residue, remember the gift of baptism as a new beginning and experience of ritual purification and initiation. Let your shower be a reminder of baptism, much the way holy water fonts invite us into a similar remembrance.

Again, you can invite in an awareness of imagery or somatic feeling into your prayer experience. When you say "sacrament," what colors or shapes do you see? How does your body feel and respond? Similarly, when you say "baptism," what images come? In what ways do you experience this in your body-being?

You might also connect the experience of the shower to your breath by staying present to how your shower fills you and helps you to release. What are the gifts—perhaps wonder, delight, relief, soothing, cleaning—the shower brings that you can inhale? What are the things the shower helps you to let go of—dirt, tension, worry—that you can exhale?

Whether your showers tend to last two minutes or twenty, continue for the duration of the experience to align your breathing with this prayer. Deepen into its meaning for you as you continue to wash clean. What are you being purified for this day? What are you being initiated into now?

Continue the breath prayer until you are no longer saying the words, but the prayer is praying through you. You might feel the sacramentality of this moment, you might know the renewal being offered to you again and again. This can be one of the gifts of memorization; the words eventually are so knit into your thoughts that there is not as much of an effort in saying them. They begin to carry you into the prayer rather than you having to try and remember what they are and directing the prayer.

On the other hand, some days you may just be repeating the words and not experiencing anything remotely like what you would consider prayer. Maybe the words feel dry and distant. Perhaps your heart and your body don't resonate with them on a given day. These are the days that are most vital to continue your practice. We don't pray only when inspired but continue to show up in all the seasons of our humanity. Some days the shower will feel like the sacrament and gift that it is, other days it may be an effort to get into the shower and prepare for the day ahead. On these difficult days, you might consider simplifying your prayer and perhaps only saying *sacrament* on the inhale and *baptism* on the exhale. Or, instead of saying the words, just holding an image for each with each breath you take, so that you continue to invite in that presence and awareness.

Some days it may be enough just to keep an awareness of the rhythm of the in-breath and the out-breath without attaching any words or images. This is the foundation of the practice and always a fruitful place to return to when doing more feels burdensome or dry and rote.

Scent brings gladness,
warmth brings comfort,
steam ascends like prayer,
taste, a doorway to awakening.

morning coffee or tea

One of my favorite times of the day is after awakening each morning. My sweet dog Sourney sleeps in bed with me and my rising kindles her excitement. I feed her and let her out. Then I brew a cup of chai tea, which I like with plenty of cream and sweetness. I love the magic of brewing—hot water poured over tea and spices, or coffee, creates something new. I allow time for it to infuse, for the botanicals to permeate the water and become tea.

I bring it back to bed with me and my little black dog follows, hops back onto the bed, and snuggles in next to me. I might spend some time journaling or more often just being quiet while slowly sipping and rubbing her belly. My warm drink ignites all of my senses and reminds me of the joys of an embodied life.

I am reminded of the monastics across time who see these morning moments as a threshold, when our awareness of the sacred becomes keener, and we are invited to whisper that universal prayer of thank you, thank you, thank you. I see this daily ritual as more than just a beverage. With presence and awareness, it becomes a doorway into gratitude for the gift of taste, touch, sight, smell, and sound. In ancient tradition, it was believed that there were five spiritual senses to mirror the five physical ones. We each have spiritual sight and hearing, spiritual smell, taste, and touch. If the senses are the way we directly experience an incarnate divine presence, then it makes sense that our senses reveal more to us than what is on the surface of things. When we pray with our sense experience, we can see how they open us up to a rich way of encountering the sacred.

We are expanding our prayer this time to four lines to remember and align with our breathing. On the inhalation, say *Scent brings gladness*, and breathe in the aroma of what you are drinking. Let the scent wash over you and bring a sense of delight.

On your exhalation, say *warmth brings comfort*, and feel the warmth of the cup in your hands. Be present to it as it radiates outward.

On your next inhale, say *steam ascends like prayer*, and you can both inhale some of the steam (being careful not to burn yourself!) and also watch it rise into the air above you. Imagine your prayers being carried on the steam into the heavens.

On your next exhale, say *taste a doorway to awakening*, and then take a sip and slowly savor it on your tongue. As you swallow, feel the warmth slide down your throat.

Notice how the experience brings you more present to life and helps to awaken your senses.

After these two breaths, you might just pause for a moment in between and listen for any sounds you hear. It could be the sound of silence and stillness, or perhaps the sound of your own breath or heartbeat. I like to listen to Sourney's breathing for a moment and feel myself connected to her in this way. Sometimes I listen for the wind or rain against my windows (I do live in Ireland, so there are many opportunities for this!).

This breath prayer practice is a particularly potent way to bring in the gift of our senses into prayer as well. The more we bring our attention to each sense experience with gratitude, the more we ground ourselves in a way of being in the world that takes our senses seriously as a doorway to the divine, much in the way our breath can.

Returning to the breath prayer, you might also want to bring in imagery as you pray, or honor the images already arising for you. This time as you inhale and pray the words *scent brings gladness*, see what images arise as you allow yourself to take in the full smell of your drink. Notice how your body responds to it.

As you exhale and pray the words *warmth brings comfort*, see what images arise in response to the feeling of warmth. What is the felt quality of warmth in your hands in the rest of your body? What does true comfort feel like?

As you inhale again and pray the words *steam ascends like prayer*, watch the wisps rise up and let yourself experience the dance it creates in your own body.

As you exhale again and pray the words *taste a doorway to awakening*, notice if the flavor brings to mind any images or colors or patterns. Pay attention to how your body reacts to the touch and taste of the brew on your tongue.

Sometimes imagery or felt experience can help root the prayer in our memories in a deeper way. Learning something by heart often means learning it through the senses so that we begin to associate certain images or feeling qualities with the words, and our bodies can then carry the prayer for us.

Adorning myself
with love and freedom.

getting dressed

Getting dressed is sometimes a straightforward act. We find something in our closets or drawers that suits what our plans are for the day. We perhaps dress nicely for work, put on workout clothes for a walk, get into our pyjamas at the end of the day. Or maybe we are going on a special date or to a celebration and we choose to dress really nicely, adding jewelry and other adornments. We dress largely in response to what activities we plan to engage in, so it demands some anticipation and planning. Clothes do say something about us. Sometimes we get dressed and don't like how we look in something, so we change our clothes to find a better fit or ensemble.

Sometimes I wish I could just wear a monk's robe day to day and keep my dressing as simple as possible. When Francis of Assisi rejected his father's wealth, he stripped naked in the public square. St. Hildegard of Bingen used to have her nuns wear beautiful jewels because she believed that they reflected interior qualities of the spirit. Those who are in mourning traditionally wore black, and a bride in the Western world traditionally wears a white dress. Clothing (or as with Francis, the lack of it) has the potential to express so much about us.

Some people are obsessed with clothing labels, while some folks love to wear the jerseys and colors of their favorite sports teams. Some hate having to wear a tie every day to their office job. One of the things I love about working from home is that I can wear pyjamas all day if I choose to. My mother used to love adorning herself with beautiful hats, scarves, and necklaces. In the later years of her life, she had to use an electric wheelchair for mobility but decided she was not going to become invisible as many people with disabilities are. For her, clothing and adornment were a way of claiming space in the world and feeling beautiful while doing it.

Sometimes clothing can be liberation and sometimes clothing can be restriction. There are ethical questions in how we get dressed too. We need to be mindful of how our clothing was produced as there is rampant use of sweatshop labor around the world. The abundance of cheap clothing has been a contributing factor to our environmental crisis. Getting dressed can be more complicated than it first appears.

Most importantly, we might ask ourselves when we get dressed if our clothing reflects who we are and what we value. We can reflect on whether getting dressed feels burdensome or pleasurable. Am I following a trend or trying to mold to cultural expectations? And does my body adornment and clothing create suffering for others?

Our breath prayer then becomes an opportunity to be fully present to our choices when getting dressed, and praying for it can be an act of both love and freedom. Love, in that the clothes we buy cause the least harm possible; freedom, in that the clothing we buy reflects something about us and isn't just an effort to look like some externally imposed standard of beauty.

You can pray this prayer as you stand in front of your closet or drawer, deciding what to choose. You can pray it as you are putting your clothing on, feeling the slide of fabric over your skin. You can take in your image in the mirror appreciating your choices of color and style or simplicity.

Breathe in: *Adorning myself*
Breathe out: *with love and freedom.*

As you inhale, become aware of how getting dressed can be an act of adornment, a way of expressing who you are or a way to prepare for which activities you are about to engage in. As you exhale, hold this intention of love and freedom, noticing what images arise as well as any bodily sensations you experience. Let this be a prayer of appreciation and awareness. This breath prayer can be as true as when we put on a sweatshirt and elastic-waist pants as when we dress up for a night out.

Look with eyes of love.
See the wholeness you are.

beholding yourself in a mirror

Many of us might have a fraught relationship to the mirror. We live in a culture of intense physical scrutiny of our perceived flaws. In an economy dependent on rampant consumerism and endless self-improvement projects, our insecurities are often amplified to sell us something. We are encouraged to dissect ourselves into parts—do we like our thighs, our belly, our nose, our chin? What can we buy to make them appear more beautiful or pleasing?

How often do we catch a glimpse of ourselves in the reflection of a window or mirror and immediately have critical thoughts about ourselves? Do we scan our bodies for imperfections in those moments?

Breathe in: *Look with eyes of love.*
Breathe out: *See the wholeness you are.*

What if we made a practice of blessing our bodies each time we looked in a mirror instead? Gazing at ourselves with kindness and compassion can be a healing journey. The next time you look in the mirror, breathe in and whisper to yourself, *Look with eyes of love*, then breathe out and say, *See the wholeness you are*. Repeat this at least three times each time you are in front of your reflection and see if you can take in the invitation offered.

This would make a rich daily practice, to make time to sit or stand in front of a mirror and instead of examining our flaws, breathing slowly while meditating on these words.

Look with eyes of love is an invitation to a kind of holy gazing. We spend much of our lives looking at the world for information to process. Gazing is a different kind of seeing, one where we look with the "eyes of your heart," an image that St. Paul uses in his letter to the Ephesians. I use this image a great deal when teaching about contemplative photography. Much of our language around cameras is quite aggressive—taking, shooting, capturing—and I invite people to consider waiting and receiving images that come as gifts instead. In a similar way, when we look in the mirror, instead of immediately trying to assess our shortcomings, we can pause, breathe deeply, and allow time to gaze upon ourselves with love. The eyes of the heart are eyes that see with wonder the gifts the world offers so freely. Can you connect to a time in your life when you were able to look unselfconsciously in the mirror?

Gazing is the kind of looking that is used when contemplating an icon, those sacred artworks that offer images of the divine and holy men and women. The mirror can become our own icon, a reflection of one who was created in the image and likeness of the divine source of all things. We can cultivate a reverence through this simple daily act of prayer. What does looking upon yourself with eyes of love evoke for you? Sometimes there can be awkwardness, as we are so unused to taking this perspective. Sometimes there is grief for the years we have spent criticizing and judging ourselves. There can be joy at starting the journey back home to ourselves again.

What a countercultural stance this could be, to practice daily looking upon ourselves with love and grace, to see ourselves as the beautiful and whole beings we already are. If you are somewhat obsessed with always trying to improve your physical appearance, consider making time each day for this breath prayer. Notice what happens when you show up for yourself in this way day after day. Do the critical voices soften? Do you feel kinder toward yourself?

With each bite, praise,
with each swallow, thanks.
May this food nourish me
so I can nourish others.

eating and savoring

Meal blessings are a part of many cultures, a practice of giving thanks for the gift of food and nourishment in our lives. We need to eat to survive, but food is also a source of pleasure and comfort, connection to others, and connection to culture and traditions. We eat to feast and celebrate. We eat to cultivate community.

So often when we eat, we forget the great pilgrimage each part of our meal made to arrive at our table. From the farmers who grew it, to those who help package and distribute it, to those who stock the shelves of the market. Seeing their sleek packaging, we can forget this ordinary miracle: the origin of things, and all of the labor involved.

We also forget the ways that eating a meal with intention and loving care, whether by ourselves or with others, nourishes us on many levels, not just the physical. Preparing and hosting a meal for another is an act of loving hospitality. The conversations that emerge over the dining table weave us together. We may remember special meals past as a taste of the heavenly banquet.

One of my favorite meals was in 1989 when I was living in Paris for a semester, studying abroad. My mother's friend knew a family who lived outside Paris and connected me with them. They invited me over to their house one afternoon and prepared a lavish multicourse meal, very traditional in France. With each course came a different kind of wine. It was sometimes a lonely experience being in Paris at the age of nineteen, far away from family and close friends, and this meal made me feel connected in ways I hadn't yet while living there. The care and welcome extended to me is a memory that still touches me these many years later. It was a feast on so many levels.

My husband and I really enjoy cooking together. We love inviting friends over to share with us and creating space for that kind of loving welcome to others. We also enjoy eating, just the two of us, the simple meals we prepare.

Pausing before we eat to breathe several times and offer a prayer infuses our eating with meaning and connection to a greater Source. We remember our vulnerability and dependence on whole systems of food production. We offer gratitude for the gift of eating and how it nourishes us so we can offer service back to the world.

Breathe in: *With each bite, praise,*
Breathe out: *with each swallow, thanks.*
Breathe in: *May this food nourish me*
Breathe out: *so I can nourish others.*

I tend to eat rather quickly. I enjoy my food but perhaps don't chew as much as would be ideal for my digestion. I find when I whisper this breath prayer in my heart while eating, it slows me down to enjoy things even more. If I say it internally while enjoying a mouthful of food, aiming not to swallow until I am done, then I can savor it even more. Breathing and slowing down our eating helps digestion too.

Pause before you begin and let the anticipation build. As you put a bite of food in your mouth and begin to chew, hold a heart of gratitude for this gift of nourishment. The breath prayer is repeated within, as eating while speaking is awkward and not recommended. As you breathe in, say quietly in your heart, *With each bite, praise*. Let yourself be filled with gratitude for all the sense experience of your food. As you breathe out, say *with each swallow, thanks* and feel the way your food moves through your body to digest and break down nutrients. Breathing in, *May this food nourish me*, breathing out, *so I can nourish others*, is a prayer of recognizing that the ways we sustain ourselves well means we can offer our gifts to the world.

Savor the experience with all of your senses—taste but also smell, textures in your mouth, sounds around you, the colors of your food. Imagine the food being digested and its nourishment traveling around your whole body.

Eating is an act of love and self-care for ourselves but also for others as it sustains us in our work in the world.

Warm water, sponge, soap,
a slow rhythm in circles,
vessels of transformation
ready to nourish again.

washing dishes

Much like the laundry, washing dishes is another of those regular tasks that can sometimes feel tedious or like drudgery. No matter how many times we wash the dishes, they pile up again and again each time we eat. Washing the dishes gives us an opportunity to feel gratitude for the meals we eat and to begin anew.

The great Spanish medieval mystic St. Teresa of Ávila said that God "walks among the pots and pans." This expressed her conviction that the kitchen is a place of holiness and grace. There is something elemental and primal about a big pot of soup warming on the stove. Our ancestors would have gathered around the hearth. Each bowlful is an act of nourishment.

The great monk St. Benedict of Nursia counselled that the kitchen utensils are as sacred as the vessels on the altar. This is a remarkable statement echoing to us from the Rule he wrote in the sixth century. Benedict considered that to be a monk was to experience everything we do as a sacred encounter.

Even with dishwashers available in most households, this act of cleaning up after a meal is another opportunity to give thanks for all the ways we have been nourished well. Scraping any excess tiny bits of food from the plates into the compost, arranging the dishes in the machine, adding the detergent and starting the cycle. This is also a threshold moment, as we prepare the dishes for their next use.

Breathe in: *Warm water, soap and sponge,*
Breathe out: *a slow rhythm in circles,*
Breathe in: *vessels of transformation*
Breathe out: *ready to nourish again.*

As you pray this breath prayer, be aware of any images or colors that arise in your imagination. Open your heart to each breath, really embracing the truth of renewal in this simple act of cleaning. Feel the warmth of the water over your hands, the pleasure you can take in moving the sponge over the plates. As you breathe, deepen your appreciation and gratitude for the ways these vessels stand ready to serve us. Even if we use a dishwasher, we can prayerfully put each plate and cup in and bless them as they are placed on the racks.

Buddhist monk Thich Nhat Hanh writes, "I enjoy taking my time with each dish, being fully aware of the dish, the water, and each movement of my hands . . . each minute and each second of life is a miracle. The dishes themselves and the fact that I am here washing them are miracles!" He sees the dishes to wash and the poems he writes and the bell ringing as all having the same value, the same potential for opening us up in this moment.

I love to consider the vessels of my life as I hold each one—a cup for my morning coffee, a bowl for the warming of soup, a glass from which to drink water, a goblet for the gladdening of wine, a plate to hold our meals, the cutlery that allows us to feed ourselves.

Most days my husband and I cook and clean just for ourselves, its own sweetness. But we especially love hosting others in our home for a slow meal and good conversation. Those dishes that remain after a sweet and satisfying evening have a special glow to them, holding the memories of connection and communal nourishment.

There is something so satisfying about returning things to order, putting them away knowing they served their specific purpose and will again serve this purpose. These vessels are renewed with each washing, waiting to renew us again as well.

An armful of towels, a pile of sheets,
an array of clothes,
simple grace of soap and water
making all things new again.

doing the laundry

L aundry, much like other forms of housecleaning, is one of those chores on endless repetition. Whether you have a large family and find yourself doing laundry almost daily, or just for yourself once a week or so, I find these moments of gathering to be powerful—the sheets from the bed, the towels from the bathroom, the clothing from the basket—they invite me to pause and reflect on my life over the previous few days and how much I take these simple pleasures of clean laundry for granted. We are embraced by these pieces of cloth, whether while sleeping at night, or after bathing, or getting dressed. They offer us warmth, protection, dryness. These materials can also be a mode of self-expression in the world.

As you walk around your home gathering the laundry, let your breath guide your pace and rhythm. Move slowly and mindfully as you create your pile of wash.

Breathe in: *An armful of towels, a pile of sheets,*
Breathe out: *an array of clothes,*

As you put the laundry into the washing machine, again let your breath slow you down to pay attention and receive the gift of what is happening.

Breathe in: *simple grace of soap and water*
Breathe out: *making all things new again.*

Allow each act of doing the laundry to become a prayer—from the gathering and separating to putting it into the washing machine, adding soap, and pressing the start button. For some, it may be washing that is done by hand, one piece of material at a time. Each aspect of doing the laundry invites us to become as present to the task at hand as we are able. I sometimes think of all the steps of doing laundry as a kind of quotidian liturgy, with its moments of preparation, culmination, and completion. Like a liturgy, each step also invites us to ponder how this task might speak to our everyday lives, and what we want to wash clean in our lives beyond the laundry. This act of prayer also calls us to a prayer of thankfulness. Each moment of the task asks us to hold gratitude for the wonder of water and soap together and the grace it offers to our lives.

This breath prayer also invites in a prayer of gratitude for all the ways that clean laundry gifts us with a fresh beginning. I love laundry days when we get the sheets and towels clean, change the bedding, and everything feels fresh. The empty laundry hamper offers a moment of newness as well, everything clean and feeling full of possibility. Perhaps the world really does begin again in these moments.

I think of the women who would have to carry laundry down to streams and rivers and wash by hand. In Ireland, they talk often about "good drying weather," a sunny day when the sheets billow like sails in the breeze.

In theologian Barbara Brown Taylor's wonderful book *An Altar in the World*, she describes hanging laundry on the line as similar to putting up prayer flags that flutter in the wind. She writes, "After a day of too much information about almost everything, there is such a blessed relief in the weight of wet clothes, causing the wicker basket to creak as I carry it out to the clothesline. . . . I hang each T-shirt like a prayer flag, shaking it first to get the wrinkles out and then pinning it to the line with two wooden clothespins."

Whether you put your laundry in the dryer after the wash or on a clothesline, this too is a part of the prayer of renewal. Buddhist author Jack Kornfield wrote a book many years ago titled *After the Ecstasy, the Laundry*. Meditation practice can bring a certain kind of freedom and transformation into our lives, one that is meant to spill over into the dailiness and the drudgery so that even the laundry becomes an opportunity for continued grace. Our breath prayer becomes an act of steadiness, a reminder of the holy in the midst of all we do.

Sacred waters,
wash me clean.
The gift of soap
to purify.

washing your hands

When the pandemic of 2020 began to spread globally, one of the first strategies promoted to help limit it was thorough handwashing for at least twenty seconds. Simple soap and water were proven to help remove it from skin surfaces. Singing the "Happy Birthday" song twice through was the older wisdom to make sure you took your time and didn't rush through the process. More recently, many new songs were suggested to entertain us while we engaged in this important task.

Handwashing is essential at all times to curb the spread of illness and disease. Many traditions have rituals around this—Christians who bless themselves with holy water, Muslims who wash their hands and feet before entering a mosque, and Jews who go to the *mikvah* for a ritual bath at prescribed times.

This act of washing our hands can become a moment of ritual, a remembrance of our purity and wholeness. It can become an opportunity to remember this act as sacred, with its roots in religious ritual and its holiness as an act of solidarity with those who are more vulnerable to illness by limiting its spread. Bring them to mind, all those with compromised immune systems and underlying conditions who benefit when we take good hygiene seriously.

If you say the breath prayer twice slowly, it takes about twenty seconds in total.

Breathe in: *Sacred waters*
Breathe out: *wash me clean.*
Breathe in: *The gift of soap*
Breathe out: *to purify.*

Pause before beginning for just a moment to transition into this act as something intentional, as a ritual of connection. Then, as you turn on the tap and take some soap, breathe in and say *Sacred waters*, then breathe out, *wash me clean*. Feel a sense of gratitude for this gift of water that flows freely into your home or workplace. As you rub your hands together think of this as an act of blessing. Feel the sensation on your skin. Handwashing is such a physical moment to reconnect with your body, to honor your body's needs.

Breathing in again, bring your awareness to the soap you are using, *The gift of soap*, breathing out, *to purify*. Scientists tell us we don't need antibacterial soap and that overuse of these products is contributing to resistant bacteria. Do you have a soap you enjoy at home, whether liquid or solid? Many people these days are making their own soap, and you can help support a local business or craftsperson by purchasing soap from them. It brings another dimension to your hand-washing ritual. Rubbing our hands with soap is enough to get them clean. Consider if there is an essential oil scent you especially love and could perhaps find soap fragranced like this. I love rosemary and peppermint as I find them invigorating, or grapefruit and other citrus, which is refreshing, or floral scents like lavender and rose, which can bring a sense of comfort.

Ritual purification is a way of honoring the fact that we long for the grace of being washed clean—whether of bacteria and viruses, or of old patterns and habits that limit us or place obstacles to our relationships with others and with the divine.

Each time we wash our hands can be a reminder, on both the physical and soul level, to wash away what blurs our vision, what keeps us from intimacy with the holy. You might add an intention as you wash your hands to purify yourself of anything that no longer serves you. You might ask: What can I release?

I witness the world's wounds,
I send forth love.
I listen
for how to respond.

reading the news

We live in a world filled with a relentless outpouring of news from all corners of the globe. It can be overwhelming to take it all in, to know how we are to respond. We can feel helpless. Often the way the news is reported is meant to divide and disempower us—amplifying extremes, featuring crisis and tragedy. Very little "good news" is reported on.

Of course, we cannot live our lives avoiding all intake of news if we're to have some sense of the issues affecting us and our communities, or be present to the suffering of others across the globe. However, being present as we take in news can be enormously helpful in keeping us from spinning out into numbness or anxiety.

We can try to find some balance in several ways.

Try making a concerted effort to follow sources of good news in the world, to celebrate the many constructive things that are also happening each day. There are websites like Yes! Magazine and The Happy Broadcast, which strive to provide information about positive steps people and governments are taking to help provide for the needs of people and the earth.

Consider creating boundaries around how much news you consume. We weren't meant to digest news all day, every day. Our minds aren't capable of processing the magnitude of what we receive on a given day. When we limit our news intake to one or two distinct periods during the day, and we make efforts to breathe and stay connected to our bodies, we are much less likely to get overwhelmed. We can also try to focus more on local news, which will impact us more directly and we have the potential of making an impact in return.

We can discern what is ours to respond to and take on. This can only happen when we have daily time to sit in stillness and drop within to listen to how we are being called. While we may wish we could respond concretely to all of the suffering on the planet, we need to return daily to what our specific gifts are and how we are able to offer them to others.

Before and after I sit down to read news, I try to center myself with my breathing and offer a prayer. This breath prayer invites me to become present as a loving witness who listens carefully for the best way to respond. Allow a few moments just to sit in silence and then repeat this breath prayer several times before starting to take in the events of the day.

Breathe in: *I witness the world's wounds*,
Breathe out: *I send forth love*.

Breathe in: *I listen*
Breathe out: *for how to respond.*

As you breathe in and say *I witness the world's wounds*, see yourself as a witness, a compassionate observer of what is happening. As you breathe out, say *I send forth love*. See this love emanating from you, see what color it is, imagine it being sent to all the hurting corners of the globe.

Then, breathing in, say *I listen*, breathing out, say *for how to respond*. This part of the prayer is another slowing down and moving intentionally out of reactivity or overwhelm. I pause and listen for the response called forth from me. Perhaps it is praying for the situation. Maybe it is donating money or writing an email. Maybe it is more direct and active involvement, or maybe simply trusting that the work you are doing is bringing loving kindness to the world.

Breathing this prayer before and after engaging with the news can slow us down enough to be present in a different way. Getting overwhelmed doesn't serve anyone and disempowers us from taking kind, simple, positive, heart-led, and just action.

Bless this portal,
thankful for ease.

working at the computer

When I was a young child, one of my most distinct memories is my mother sitting at her typewriter writing her doctoral dissertation. There was the loud clacking sound the keys made, the rolling of the paper in and out, the ring when she got to the end of a line and hit the return key. I remember the strong smell of correction fluid she would spread thinly on the page to correct any errors. I remember the piles of edited pages scribbled with red writing through the margins and her dutifully retyping them all again.

I also remember our art encyclopedia set. My father was from Austria, so we had a set of books in German that covered art from many different eras. The entries were of particular artist names as well as styles. Both my parents always had a great love and appreciation for art so were often pulling one of these volumes off the shelf to look something up or just to enjoy the images.

Even though I lived for more than twenty years in a pretechnological world, it is hard to remember now sometimes how different things were before computers and mobile devices became so widely accessible. Now we rely on them all the time for information, communication, work. As a writer who spends many hours at my computer each week, I am profoundly grateful to only have to type out my words once and not retype whole pages with each round of editing.

I am also grateful for the immense amount of information available to me with a few keystrokes. From science to art to news to the natural world, there is so much available to me in word and image almost immediately. No heavy books on the shelves or trips to the library for research.

Because it is so easy to forget this could be otherwise, I like to pause every so often and feel gratitude and appreciation for the gift of ease technology brings to my life. I think of this breath prayer as a mini-blessing in the moment to help me to remember.

Breathe in: *Bless this portal,*
Breathe out: *thankful for ease.*

This prayer might feel especially important when we encounter an issue with our technology. We can spend hours and hours enjoying the freedom and ease our devices bring to us, but the moment they slow down, stall, or simply don't work, it can feel like our world has come undone. In those moments, I try to remember that I would still rather deal with the issues that arise than go back to life pretechnology.

Breathing in, imagine you are blessing the computer. See it as the portal it is to a huge world of information. As you breathe out, feel a deep sense of gratitude for the ease it brings to your life.

Whether you use a computer for work or writing or home finances, whether you use your mobile device to track messages, the weather, the time, your calendar, or any number of other functions, pause on occasion to appreciate the blessing that this is. Bringing presence to our use of devices can also help us not to use them as mindlessly as we often do. It supports us in being mindful processors of information and also in knowing when it is time to shut the computer or tablet or phone off for a while and plug into the world beyond screens.

Let this be a vessel for connection,
bringing me fully present.

checking your phone

How many times a day do you check your phone? If you're anything like me, you might not even be able to count because it happens so many times, and often so mindlessly. It used to be that the phone was just for making and receiving calls; we would never have thought to pick it up to just look at it. Even when we added mobility and text capability, we'd only pick it up when we needed to make or receive a call or send a message.

Now we are connected to email, work, apps, social media, a constant stream of news, games, films, and other entertainment. There is so much good that technology brings to our lives, but its shadow side is how much time and energy it steals from us when we allow it. It is so easy to forget why you even picked up your phone in the first place as you go down another rabbit hole of information.

We do not need to demonize our phones or technology, we simply need to bring more awareness to our time spent with devices. A prayer is a way to bring gratitude for the many gifts it brings and also mindfulness about when we are just bored and looking for distraction.

Breathe in: *Let this be a vessel for connection*,
Breathe out: *bringing me fully present*.

This breath prayer invites us to remember how we want (and do not want) to use our mobile devices. When we bring the intention of letting it connect us to others and the world, and recognize when time spent on it moves to a place of distraction or numbness, we can become more mindful about how we engage technology.

Breathe in: *Let this be a vessel for connection*,
Breathe out: *bringing me fully present*.

As you repeat this prayer to yourself, notice if there are any images that arise when you breathe in a sense of connection. Similarly, notice what arises when you breathe out presence and release any numbing or avoidance. Let yourself drop deeply into this rhythm of embracing connection and releasing numbness. You might even simplify the prayer so that when you breathe in, gently say to yourself *connect*, and when you breathe out say *presence*, while holding an image of release that comes naturally with the exhalation.

I find that boundaries around my screen time really nourish me well. I try to put my phone in a drawer at night so I am not tempted to reach for it if I awaken in the middle of the night. I can also allow myself some time before trying to sleep where I read or journal without screens and the same thing when I first awaken. I love those quiet threshold moments between sleeping and awakening for meditation and presence.

These kinds of boundaries help me to remember that I am not at the mercy of other people's demands on my time and attention. Because I work for myself, there is always something I could be doing, something I could be responding to. I imagine it is much the same even when you work for someone else. How many of us feel the need to always be available?

In his poem "How to Be a Poet," Wendell Berry gives advice to "stay away from screens." The poetry of life most often is revealed through engagement with what feels real, what we experience through our senses.

I wouldn't want to be without the gift of technology and yet it is also what exhausts me the most. Bringing my breath and prayerful attention to how I engage with it allows it to be life-giving rather than draining.

May my words
be kind and true,
connecting
and encouraging.

sending an email or text

How many times a day do we communicate via technology? I would not be able to count the number of emails or other messages I respond to in a given day. It seems there are more and more ways to communicate: email, text, messages that come through other apps like WhatsApp, Facebook, Instagram, and Twitter. It can be tempting to rush through this communication and get it done as quickly as possible. Yet there is an opportunity here to make our communications full of lovingkindness, no matter who we are writing or responding to.

I've been on the receiving end of messages that feel cold, tense—even hostile. I am sure I have sent messages like this myself when I am feeling tired or hurt or angry, or just stressed by the demands on my time and the weight of all that harms the earth and threatens its communities. Breath prayer can be an extra gift to lean into when we have a difficult email to write and want our communication to respect the dignity of those we are writing to, not cause further harm.

In our daily communications, we have an opportunity and invitation to pause and consider how we interact with others, especially in that strange realm of technology where tone and body language are almost impossible to detect.

Perhaps some messages just call for a quick yes or no and don't require long pauses of presence. But especially when you feel any kind of emotional charge while writing, or you have been writing what feels like too many messages already, it can be helpful to call upon our breath prayer to support us in refocusing our attention and awareness.

If you are replying to hundreds of messages a day, especially as part of a work requirement, it may not be possible to pause and breathe for several minutes before each one. But it might be possible to take two slow deep breaths and repeat this prayer to yourself:

Breathe in: *May my words*
Breathe out: *be kind and true,*
Breathe in: *connecting*
Breathe out: *and encouraging.*

Kindness is a very underrated quality in this world. Yet I can think of many moments in my own life when I was deeply touched and uplifted in a difficult time simply because of the kindness of another. It might be a kind message that arrives to my inbox, letting me know how much my work means to them. Or it might be the cashier in the grocery store who smiles at me, doesn't seem rushed at all, and asks how my day is going in a sincere way.

I can pause and, in this breath prayer, ask myself if my message is kind, true, connecting, and encouraging. Does my message dismiss the other person's concern in any way? Is it passive-aggressive? Is it curt and cold in tone?

Loving communication helps to make the world a gentler place. Pausing during our emails helps them to become less of a task and a chore and more of a way to be present to others.

It may seem counterintuitive, but the more we pause and breathe when feeling overburdened, the more inner space we create and the more centered we become. Rather than rushing through our tasks, presence helps us to feel more expansive in our days and brings gentleness to our connections with others.

Scrub the toilet, sink
and shower tiles.
An act of love
making all things new

cleaning the bathroom

I don't particularly enjoy housecleaning. I love the result of it, but often when it is just my husband and me at home alone, it gets forgotten or avoided until things really need cleaning. Perhaps when a guest is coming.

I very much enjoy inviting guests into our home for dinner or a games night or a cup of tea and conversation. When we invite others in, I become more aware of what needs cleaning and it becomes an act of hospitality. Suddenly scrubbing the bathroom becomes an act of loving care, to prepare the space for another.

Sometimes I can even be present enough to enjoy the process for myself. To realize how I am extending hospitality and loving care by keeping things clean and looking fresh. When I remember to practice a prayer of presence, the task can be transformed into something different, similar to how I feel when I do it to welcome others. I can rediscover the grace in this simple act of cleaning.

Breathe in: *Scrub the toilet, sink*
Breathe out: *and shower tiles.*

Breathe in: *An act of love*
Breathe out: *making all things new*

With my first breath cycle, I bring myself fully present to the physical act of cleaning and scrubbing. With my second breath cycle, I honor how this act can offer a gift to myself and others. When we bring our full attention to what we are doing, we can discover in the heart of this act a bringing to clarity and making things new again. Our lives are a continual cycle of things getting dirty—dishes, clothing, bathrooms, kitchens—and showing up over and over to clean them. This repetition can become its own kind of meditation on the cyclical rhythm of our lives.

In these moments, the wisdom of Buddhist teacher Thich Nhat Hanh reminds me: "Don't do any task in order to get it over with. Resolve to do each job in a relaxed way, with all your attention. Enjoy and be one with your work."

Bathrooms are areas of private acts—eliminating, washing, and grooming. They offer us a space to show up in the world, where we can take care of our physical needs and practice good hygiene. It is an important space for our lives, and when I remember this, I am more present to cleaning as an important process, as an act of meditation. My breath brings me to this moment now. And as I breathe into this prayer and in this space, I experience gratitude for this opportunity.

*I watch your belly
rise and fall.
"The breathing together
of all things."*

holding a dog or cat in your lap

Some of my most treasured moments of the day are when my dog Sourney, a rescued Patterdale terrier, comes to nuzzle in beside me in bed or on the sofa. She either curls up in a little ball with her chin on my leg or stretches her body long, revealing her chest to me, guiding my hand there with her paw. Perhaps you have a companion animal of some kind, a dog or a cat or even a rabbit or guinea pig.

You are invited to make time each day to just sit and breathe with them, to connect your breath to their breath and feel the profundity of this human-animal connection, and to feel yourself connected to the wider creation through them. If you slow yourself down enough you can feel a connection to all of creation through this simple act of breathing. Simply watch their belly's movements in synchrony with their breath as a meditation on this beautiful dance happening all at once. Place your hand on their belly to feel those sacred rhythms. As you enter into breath prayer with them, try to match the pace of your breathing to theirs.

Breathe in: *I watch your belly*
Breathe out: *rise and fall.*
Breathe in: *"The breathing together*
Breathe out: *of all things."*

The first part of the breath prayer is simply watching, attending, feeling this deep connection. Watch with wonder at the belly's slow rise and fall, this miracle of fur and love and how life moves through them moment by moment.

The second part of the breath prayer, uttering the phrase "the breathing together of all things," comes from the paleontologist and spiritual writer Pierre Teilhard de Chardin, who used this phrase to describe how everything is interconnected. Each time we exhale, trees take in the carbon dioxide we expel and transform it into oxygen. They expel the oxygen for us and other creatures to take in. This is a magnificent dance. It is in these quiet moments that I can feel this breathing together, and it makes me feel expansive, connected, reverent. While this breath prayer is about cats and dogs, it might be expanded to creatures, trees and growing plants, wind, the elements.

While Sourney is most definitely a domesticated animal and not a creature of the wilds, I also love the sense of my connection to the instinctual mind in these moments. She follows her own desires and inclinations as the day unfolds rather than a predetermined schedule. Being present to her in this way helps me to consider how I connect to my own instinctual being and live from a place of more spontaneous honoring of my needs rather than habits or patterns of doing. This is another layer of presence and curiosity you can bring to this prayer practice.

Many of us experience the profound joy at the unconditional love our companion animals provide to us. We never have to fear judgment from them and they are always present, no matter what else is going on in the world. Their abiding love is a balm in difficult moments.

Bless the flow of resources
in and out of my life.
Give me
a generous heart.

balancing your finances

Sometimes balancing the finances can be overwhelming. No matter where we are in life, financial stressors are often an everyday experience. Living paycheck to paycheck, finding yourself unemployed, and meeting your or your family's basic needs can all induce anxiety.

For us, being self-employed means we are fully responsible for our income and funding things like health insurance, sick days, vacation time, and retirement planning. Anytime there is a dip in income, stress and worry can rise up.

Then there is the drain of expenses, especially the unexpected ones when something needs replacing, or paying taxes. All of us face that. There are important things that taxes support: communal funds to build roads and hospitals, support for public transit, support for the disabled and unemployed, and pay for education and schools, among other valuable things. But the tedium and complexity of calculating taxes and gathering forms and filing taxes for an annual return can leave a person less than enchanted. And the monthly demands of meeting bills brings its own challenges.

We might try to shift our perspective on tasks we find onerous or overwhelming by beginning the finance time with a prayer of gratitude. When we have enough to meet our bills, it is indeed a privilege. To acknowledge an income, and offer gratitude for work that provides the basics. It is also a blessing for those of us who have a home, with water and electricity and a refrigerator with food, and to be able to donate money and time to important causes. For many of us, our needs are simple (shelter, water, food). When those needs are met, it's cause for gratitude.

This act of pausing allows us to bring an important shift in perspective so that we can move from a sense that many of us feel of drudgery or overwhelm to a place of presence and blessing. Pausing helps us remember the many gifts this act of balancing money is accounting for.

You might say this prayer several times with your breath to bring yourself present to the gift of resources, to remember the call to be generous with what you have, to not hold on too tightly.

Pausing helps connect me with others who rest in that space of unknowing what the future will bring, especially when times are tight or emergencies happen. In these moments especially, I am in solidarity with that human experience of vulnerability and am attentive to those in need around me.

In my better moments I let balancing my finances be a ritual I do when I am feeling well. I try not to be tired or hungry when I sit down, and I breathe deeply as I work, pausing regularly to offer my breath prayer.

Breathe in: *Bless the flow of resources*
Breathe out: *in and out of my life.*
Breathe in: *Give me*
Breathe out: *a generous heart.*

I begin by blessing this flow of money and how it moves both into and out of my account and my life. For all the income I receive for my work, there are the things I spend money on. Sometimes these are essentials like home, food, utilities, and medicine. Sometimes we decide it is time for new clothing, or books for research, or I might sign up for an art class. Other times it may be a long-awaited trip or a spontaneous dinner out for a date night or celebration.

This flow in and out is a necessary one. We each require income to sustain ourselves and then what we spend money on helps to sustain others.

The second part of this breath prayer is a prayer for generosity. Rather than having our finances create a sense of grasping or contracting in us, we might ask, Can it expand me outward? For every little treat or splurge on myself, I ask: Can I be intentional in contributing in some way to the well-being of others? Even in times of financial hardship, asking: Can I cultivate a posture of generosity to the world, receiving gifts in whatever form they might arrive? When there is great need, am I able to contribute something of the gifts I have received?

I bring myself here and now.
I will arrive in good time.

running late

I hate being late. I especially hate the rushed, anxious feeling I get when I realize I won't arrive somewhere on time—whether due to my own fault or other delays along the way. I hate disappointing people and keeping them waiting.

But I have learned that the fret and worry will not move me along any more quickly than I am moving already. Getting angry or frustrated just means I arrive late *and* I feel out of sorts, not centered or fully present. So then I am not only keeping someone waiting, but I arrive feeling scattered and distracted, not able to be fully present to them.

When you find yourself stuck in traffic or another situation where you know you are going to be delayed, after sending a message to the person waiting for you, accept the invitation to breathe.

Breathe in: *I bring myself here and now.*
Breathe out: *I will arrive in good time.*

With your inhale, try to be as present to this moment as possible. With your exhale, try to release any worries and anxieties, knowing that you have no control over the situation other than your response. All you can do is trust that you will arrive safely.

You will arrive in good time, which means it might not be the time you had wanted or planned to arrive—it might even mean you miss something altogether (depending on how late you actually are), but you give yourself grace in these moments, knowing nothing will change by your growing frustration.

You might think of the white rabbit in *Alice in Wonderland* who is always lamenting, "I'm late, I'm late, for a very important date." The rabbit is always rushing off somewhere. If we find ourselves often running late, we might start to ask ourselves if our lives are overscheduled. Perhaps we are trying to fit in too many things into the time we have. Sometimes we move through our lives breathlessly from one commitment to another and never have the time to either integrate what has happened or to consider if we want to keep this pace up for ourselves.

Many of us think that if we just had more hours in the day, we would be able to get all of our tasks done. And yet the challenge isn't that we need to do more but that we need to be able to pause and show up fully for the moments we are currently rushing through. Even those frustrating times when we are running late and start to feel the urgency of time more keenly are their own invitation for us to pay attention.

In those moments, breathing and praying help to create a bit of spaciousness and a window into a new way of being in the world.

sanctifying time

I step into night's dark cave,
imagine Earth holding my worries.
I release into the mystery of sleep
and wisdom of dreams.

bedtime

I am someone who loves the dark hours of the night. In the summer in Ireland, those contract to very few, and close to the summer solstice the sun sets after I go to bed and rises before I awaken. But the winter is very different, the sky grows dark by late afternoon and usually I wake up in time to see the sun slowly light up the sky. It is a sweet time of candles and reading, snuggling inside with my journal.

To me, rest and sleep are precious and celebrated. I have an autoimmune illness, which means I have to get a lot of sleep to function well. I appreciate the symbols that arise in my dreams at night, bringing me insight into waking life choices.

Western culture has a difficult relationship to darkness and winter. As a culture, we value productivity and doing, so to slow down and rest can be challenging. We try to illuminate all the dark corners of our life with electric lights and screens. Yet darkness can be fertile, like the womb we all emerged from. Winter is the time of hibernation and incubation, when creative seeds begin to take root deep under the earth long before they are visible above ground. So many of us are exhausted, stretched thin by too many demands and struggling with insomnia for various reasons.

We can reclaim bedtime as a gift. We can approach the growing darkness as a time to set aside our plans and agendas and let go into the restorative cocoon of sleep. We can remember that this time of day is as essential to our thriving as our daytime doing is.

In the monastic tradition, Compline is the last prayer of the day, the time of entering the Great Silence. Monastics keep silence all through the night as a way to honor night's mystery and give space for the deep rest we are all invited to participate in. Our days can be so busy that night is often the only time when we can offer ourselves a holy pause from our relentless doing.

Night calls us to wordlessness and unknowing. We live in a world where we can shop and entertain ourselves online or answer emails 24/7, so it takes a special kind of commitment and vigilance to guard these dark hours for ourselves so that we might be deeply renewed and restored for the important work of our lives.

Breathe in: *I step into night's dark cave,*
Breathe out: *imagine Earth holding my worries.*
Breathe in: *I release into the mystery of sleep*
Breathe out: *and wisdom of dreams.*

Consider creating a short ritual for bedtime. Put your phone and tablet away from your bed. Sit and breathe for several minutes while repeating this breath prayer to yourself. Notice your body's response to these words of letting go and surrender. See if you might bring your breath to places of holding and tightness and allow yourself to physically soften a bit more. This softening of the body helps the mind and the spirit to soften as well, to recognize they don't have to hold on so tightly for a while.

See yourself stepping into the dark cave of night as a space of sanctuary and holding, a cocoon for deep rest and renewal. Imagine you can give your worries and pain over, as the poet Rainer Maria Rilke wrote: "Let its weight fall back into the earth."

This breath prayer is a prayer of intentional letting go. We allow Earth to hold anything that worries or concerns us or brings us anxiety. We allow ourselves to release into the mysteries of the dark hours of the day, yielding to a place of rest and renewal.

This time of day echoes the energies of autumn moving into winter, a time to let go and release whatever has its hold on us, a time to honor that we do not know how the seeds within us will take shape against the morning sky.

I surrender the ache,
and the worry.
Breathe in stillness,
breathe out anxiety.

waking in the middle of the night

Intentionally, in the middle of the night, monastics used to awaken to pray Vigil. Some of the stricter monastic orders still do. It is a way of consecrating all the hours of the day, including the dark of the night.

If our sleep patterns get disrupted and we awaken sometime in those early hours before the sun rises, we might consider joining those ancient contemplatives in our imaginations and with prayer. Rather than get hooked into the anxiety of our churning thoughts, this opening to the night can be an opportunity to savor stillness, to rest into the unknown, to breathe love out to a hurting world, to bathe our communities in prayers for peace, and to allow our breathing to soften our hold on things so that we might slowly release ourselves back into slumber.

For me, the worst anxiety can come when I have to be somewhere the next day, perhaps teaching in the morning, and I start to worry whether I will get enough rest. This worry, of course, interferes with the possibility of going back to sleep and can become a vicious cycle.

Sometimes I sit up and read for a while or write down what I think my mind is grasping for. But mostly breath

127

and prayer are the balm that help to calm and soothe me. They help to sanctify these moments when I would prefer to be asleep. They become opportunities for prayer and connection with Source. I see myself joining with monks around the world awake at that very same moment, offering their prayers of praise and gratitude.

Breathe in: *I surrender the ache,*
Breathe out: *and the worry.*
Breathe in: *Breathe in stillness,*
Breathe out: *breathe out anxiety.*

Similar to the breath prayer at bedtime, this breath prayer is about allowing our body to surrender and yield, to release anxiety and worry as much as possible, and let the darkness comfort and hold us for a while. This time of night wakefulness can be a practice in learning to appreciate mystery. So much of the anxiety arises from the parts of ourselves that want to plan and control and know the outcome of things. Of course, none of us knows these things, and life is largely out of our control.

In the first part of the breath prayer, see if you can physically allow your body to surrender anything it is holding onto. Sometimes taking an extra deep breath and letting it out with a long sigh can really help with this release.

In the second part of the breath prayer, notice what breathing in stillness and breathing out anxiety feel like for you. See what colors or sensations are present. If it is helpful to pray with images, visualize your inhale drawing in this gift of stillness. Visualize your exhale letting go of any anxiety or worry.

In his poem "Sweet Darkness," David Whyte writes, "The night will give you a horizon / further than you can see." Many of us aren't used to spending time with ourselves, and when we slow down and let go of the many possible distractions we are left with our mind's churning. Breath prayer helps us to ease the racing thoughts by giving our mind another focus and direction. We can bring an intention of restfulness and release to our nighttime hours though this practice. The words provide us with an intention so we might find more ease in these middle-of-the-night awakenings.

I begin this work
with a focused heart,
grateful
to be of service.

start of the workday

In our modern culture, we live with extremes about work. Some disparage work and live for Fridays (TGIF) and weekends. Some are working in jobs that are difficult and demanding and they deal with internal struggle on meeting the challenges. Some are in a time of their life when they are looking for work, which is sometimes the hardest work. Certainly work doesn't always feel meaningful or valued. Many people are just trying to get through their days. And some live by holding the dream of retirement. It is unfortunate we have such a challenging relationship to something we spend so many hours of our lives doing.

In the Benedictine tradition, work and prayer are at the heart of the monk's day. The ability to work and provide for oneself is greatly valued. For some of us, our paid work isn't necessarily what we consider our vocation or calling. Sometimes we do our true work in our off hours, whether as a volunteer, or gardening in our yard, or creating something at our kitchen table.

Joan Chittister, an author and Benedictine sister, writes in praise of work:

The implications of a spirituality of work in a world such as ours are clear, it seems. Work is my gift to the world. It is my social fruitfulness. It ties me to my neighbor and binds me to the future.

Work is the way I am saved from total self-centeredness. It gives me a reason to exist that is larger than myself. It makes me part of possibility. It gives me hope.

Even if the work we do to support ourselves isn't especially meaningful to us or fulfilling, we can still bring a heart of gratitude for the ability to work and earn a living. We can bring more kindness to those we interact with during our workday, whether coworkers or customers or clients. When the global pandemic of 2020 first arrived, we began to see how essential certain kinds of work actually is, work that is low-paid and often not valued, such as medical and service work. We can begin to see how the work we do connects us to a whole network of labor that provides for human flourishing.

If you work outside the home, see if you might arrive to your workplace just a few minutes early. Allow some time to breathe deeply and connect with the breath prayer below as a way to bless and sanctify your day.

Breathe in: *I begin this work*
Breathe out: *with a focused heart,*

The first part of this breath prayer is an act of beginning with intention. It is a way of remembering ourselves and our purpose rather than moving through the day mindlessly, simply watching the clock until we can go home.

Breathe in: *grateful*
Breathe out: *to be of service.*

The second part of this breath prayer is an act of gratitude. It is a way of remembering the gift that work can offer to us, both in terms of livelihood as well as in meaning and purpose. Whatever kind of work we do, it is always in service to something bigger than ourselves. Whether stocking grocery shelves, working at a bank, teaching a classroom, or working as an artist. Work has a way of connecting us to a whole community that needs each of us to offer our effort on its behalf.

I have found even in those moments when the work I was engaged in felt no longer nourishing to me, rather than spending each day feeling disconnected or resentful, the more I could maintain a heart of connection and gratitude, the more I was supported to listen for how I was

133

actually being called. Breath prayer can help remind us of the ways our work supports the well-being of others and how we can be of service even when it feels difficult to do so. Sometimes it means finding ways outside of work to express myself creatively, whether by taking a poetry class or volunteering at a soup kitchen. When I finished college and moved across the country to participate in the Jesuit Volunteer Corps, I spent a year working with emotionally disturbed youth. The work was certainly meaningful, but many aspects of it revealed to me how this was not what I was called to do, and that was just as valuable as knowing my gifts.

You might also consider using this breath prayer at the end of your workday and change out the word *begin* with *end* as a way to honor this transition:

I end this work
with a focused heart,
grateful
to be of service.

I pause
I breathe
I begin
again.

midway through the workday
(or midway through a work project)

In the desert tradition, *acedia* was known as the noon-day demon. Midway through the work of the day, a kind of lethargy sometimes sets in, a boredom, a sense of tedium.

It is a very human experience to start something—a workday, a project, a piece of writing—full of enthusiasm and the energy that comes from newness. But then partway through, our motivation starts to wane, our inner thoughts and judgments start to get louder, and we may start to wonder if this is really all worth the effort. We may wonder if what we are doing is any good, or whether we might as well quit while we're ahead. We each have our own version of these voices and the messages they shout to us when we start to feel tired, bored, or otherwise lacking motivation.

We perhaps make the mistake of believing that we need to be full of motivation at all times or it isn't worth the effort. We forget that we are human with all of our fluctuations in energy and desire. We wax and wane like the moon and the sea. At these moments of waning we have an invitation to recommit, to begin again. Beginning again is at the heart of the monastic path. Buddhists describe the practice of "beginner's mind" as one in which we remember that we are never masters of anything, especially life. We must commit each day anew, and we are always on a journey of discovery and transformation. In the Benedictine way, this connects to the practice of conversion. Conversion is remembering that we are never done, we are always learning, always growing.

In these moments of *acedia*, we have the opportunity to acknowledge our humility and limitations. We can renew ourselves and our commitment to our task. The desert mothers and fathers saw the opportunity to begin again in each moment.

In her book *Acedia and Me*, Benedictine oblate and author Kathleen Norris writes about her own struggle with this noonday demon and how ancient wisdom supported her:

> As a writer I must begin, again and again, at that most terrifying of places, the blank page. And as a person of faith I am always beginning again with prayer. I can never learn these things, once and for all, and master them. I can only perform them, set them aside, and then start over. Beginning requires that I remain willing to act, and to summon my hopes in the face of torpor.

In these times when our energy and enthusiasm wane, we can call upon our breath as a support and animator for our focus. Even if you have reached midway through your work day and are not feeling *acedia* settle in yet, it is still a helpful and enriching practice to recommit yourself for the rest of the day.

At your midday break, pause for five minutes of breathing and stillness and repeat these words gently to yourself.

Breathe in: *I pause*
Breathe out: *I breathe*
Breathe in: *I begin*
Breathe out: *again.*

As you repeat this breath prayer, feel both the energy of pausing as well as the energy of beginning again. Notice any images that arise for each of those inner movements. In pausing we create a little oasis of stillness. We open up a space of rest within ourselves. We can integrate what has come before, much the way in yoga practice corpse pose comes at the end of each physical practice, as an opportunity to let the body incorporate what it has experienced.

In beginning again, we acknowledge ourselves as beginners. We recognize that we will fall asleep to life again and again. We will continually return to a place of doubt or lack of effort unless we recommit ourselves. The opportunity to begin again is present in each transition we make throughout the day when we start or end each activity. There is a threshold moment there, a doorway we cross into something new when we can commit our presence and attention to the task. The middle of the workday can be an especially rich time to do this as a way to cultivate a loving awareness in all that we do.

Anytime we start to feel ourselves wane or grow weary, we can pause again for this breath prayer and begin anew.

*I light a flame
to remember
all is sacred
here and now.*

lighting a candle

The act of lighting a candle creates a shift in intention and energy of the room. Most religious traditions use candles on their altars as a symbol of divine presence or a desire for illumination. For Shabbat services every Friday evening, the candles are lit to welcome the Queen of Sabbath who bestows her gift of rest freely.

In Christian churches for Advent, each week for four weeks a new candle is added to symbolize the light growing in the darkness. In November, candles are lit in remembrance of those who have died. In churches, we light candles to represent the prayers we bring. The burdens may feel heavy at times, but fire has a way of purging and purifying.

If we want to create a special atmosphere, we dim lights and set out candles. Something about the warmth of flame, rather than a light bulb, touches a primal longing in us.

How often do we light a candle in our daily lives? There are so many opportunities—at the start of the day, as we sit down to meditate or pray, when we sit down to journal or make art, for a meal, when we take a bath, when having a conversation with a beloved one.

Consider finding time each day to light a candle—to mark your prayer time, your mealtime, bathing, or some other activity you want to sanctify. Make a commitment to this act daily—both the lighting of the candle as well as the practice it accompanies.

This simple act signals to us that we are crossing a threshold, deepening our awareness of how the sacred is present here, now, always. This is true in all moments, but certain ritual acts help us to pause and remember, to pay attention. In some ways, it is the physical equivalent of the breath prayer—a way to remember that the holy is here now. Lighting a candle simply magnifies what is already true and amplifies the prayer we say with our breath.

Your prayer each day might be simply to light a candle for five minutes and repeat the breath prayer gently to yourself during this time. Decide on when you will incorporate this practice into your daily rhythm. Find a candle you love, or a simple beeswax one will do. Begin with a few deep, quiet breaths as you light the lighter or strike the match. As you touch the flame to the wick, offer this prayer:

Breathe in: *I light a flame*
Breathe out: *to remember*
Breathe in: *all is sacred*
Breathe out: *here and now.*

Once the flame is lit, sit for several minutes just repeating this prayer while gazing on the flame. Let the flame be an anchor for your attention along with the words you are speaking. Breathing in, say *I light a flame*, breathing out, say *to remember*. The root of the word *remember* is re-member, which means to make whole again. Our loving attention and awareness remind us of our original wholeness.

Continue the prayer, breathing in, *all is sacred*, breathing out, *here and now*. The Sufi poet Hafiz writes: "Now is the time to know that all you do is sacred." And St. Benedict prompts us to remember that each moment of time is sacred, each person we encounter is sacred, and each object we interact with is sacred too.

I recommend resting into this candle-lighting breath prayer for five minutes before transitioning into whatever sacred activity you were lighting the candle to mark.

You might also call on this prayer in moments when you don't have a candle available but are in need of reminding of the sacredness of all moments. You can light a candle in your imagination, calling forth the flame of love in your heart that St. John of the Cross describes in his poetry. This flame burns perpetually, but we can make it a practice to tend it and connect with it in quiet moments so we can remember it is always present when we need it.

Feet bless the earth,
I belong here.

a walk in nature

There is nothing like a walk in the forest to rejuvenate me and help me connect again to my wild center—that place within me free from the small daily anxieties of living where I am connected to Earth through my senses. Each day our sweet dog Sourney gets excited when we reach for her leash and open the door. Most days we walk up the canal that flows by our apartment building and back down the river. These are lovely walks with very few cars and time I feel connected to water, trees, and weather. As a writer, my daily walks are an essential time to step away from my desk and the computer screen and feel the flow of movement that always seems to break open a new idea for me.

On our Sabbath days each week, we try to go a bit further afield. My favorite place to walk is Cong Woods, about a forty-five-minute drive north of us in Galway. There I am surrounded by the vibrant green of trees coated in moss.

I also love being by the sea and walking along the shoreline, feeling connected to the rhythm of waves and tides. We are lucky to live by the Atlantic, but the wind can be fierce here in the west of Ireland, especially in winter.

Some days gusts come and ask me to hold on lightly to whatever I am grasping. Some days a wild wind gives me the feeling of having things shaken loose in me, inviting me to release them.

The ancient Christian abbas and ammas left cities in search of wild places. Those in Egypt and Syria went out to the desert to find a place of radical stillness and connection to the divine presence. Those in Ireland and Scotland sought out forests and islands, edge places, where they could encounter an undomesticated God. There is a human longing for wildness, to feel ourselves connected to bark, leaves, and blooms, to those with fur and fangs, to join Earth in her ongoing prayers of praise.

Whether your walk takes you out to wilderness places, or you walk the local streets in your neighborhood, you have an opportunity to connect your breath to the rhythm of your stride and to feel yourself held by the expansiveness of sky.

Consider walking slowly, without having a destination in mind. Let the walk unfold moment by moment, listening to the invitation of the world around you to pause and savor.

Breathe in: *Feet bless the earth*,
Breathe out: *I belong here*.

Imagine that as you walk your footsteps bless the ground beneath you. Each stride you take is an act of prayer and gratitude for the ways nature supports and sustains you.

Breathe out a sense of belonging to the wider world. One of nature's gifts can be a sense of deep solace and support. A sense that we belong here, that we are a part of creation.

We breathe more deeply as we walk, our movement demanding a more vigorous rhythm. If we are fortunate to live somewhere with clean air, walking outside may bring a certain refreshment to our minds and bodies as well.

Sometimes we are trying hard to figure something out in our lives, and the greatest gift we can offer to ourselves is to let it go for a while. On my walks, insight almost always comes in one form or another. It might be the simple truth of feeling connected to the river's flow or the heron's stillness and then graceful flight. It might be a more personal truth of what I am invited to release on any given day. I find difficult emotions like anger or grief tend to soften when I allow them to be held by nature. Walking helps them move through me, so I can honor that experience without feeling stuck in them.

The poet Wallace Stevens wrote: "Perhaps the truth depends on a walk around a lake." As we walk, we are invited to shed anything untrue. We may be feeling anxious over the state of the world or of our lives, and walking has a way of returning us to ourselves and to our center. Our breath returns us to each step as a threshold to feeling more deeply rooted here and now.

I plant the seeds
that grow and bloom.
Cycles of life and death
nourished by soil, sun, and rain

gardening

I live in an apartment in an urban center and a few years ago I started growing herbs in planters on my balcony. I am fortunate to have a good bit of space out there and I started with lavender and rosemary at first, good vigorous growers, easy to maintain. Then with each new season, I started adding new ones. Marigolds grow especially well from seed, with little effort on my part; their orange and gold faces uplift my spirits. St. John's Wort loves to spread and bloom each year near the summer solstice. The rosemary grows vigorously all year long. I don't need a whole yard or acres of land to connect to Earth's rhythms of life and death.

Each morning I let my dog out on the balcony to stretch her legs and do her business (we have this wonderful invention called a porch potty, kind of like an outdoor litter box for dogs). In those moments, I greet these green growing friends. I let them speak to me of what season it is and what the invitation to me might be. I spend time noticing how they are, if they need water or perhaps are saturated from all of the rain we receive.

I speak to them as friends, as they have become such bringers of joy and companionship. Even in the midst of dark or challenging days, I can stand beside the yarrow and find comfort in her white blooms or take some mint between my fingers, break the leaves apart, and inhale deeply.

Breathe in: *I plant the seeds*
Breathe out: *that grow and bloom.*
Breathe in: *Cycles of life and death*
Breathe out: *nourished by soil, sun, and rain*

Whether you have planted the seeds yourself or bought your plant already sprouted and partially grown, these green companions connect you to this mystery of seed and growth. Whether the plants you have flower at all, they still connect you to the possibilities of blooming in every living thing.

The next part of the breath prayer roots you in an awareness of the sacred cycles and rhythms the seasons bring. Blossom, fruit, release, and rest are the movements of spring, summer, fall, and winter—both in the outer world as well as in our inner worlds. These cycles are nourished by such elemental things as soil, sun, rain—a glorious partnership in allowing life to flourish and grow. We too are nourished by these elements, the food we eat, our connection to Earth beneath our feet and the movement of the sun across the sky.

In Ireland, there is a sharp contrast between summer and winter in terms of number of daylight hours and the arc the sun makes across the sky. During summer the arc is a large circle high in the sky, while in winter the sun is confined to a low arc close to the horizon. The plants sense these rhythms and respond accordingly.

Each season is essential to the whole cycle of growth. With autumn's release of leaves, fertile compost is given back to the ground and will become nourishing soil. Sun and rain help to break down the dead materials into something life-giving. With winter's time of rest and incubation, seeds deep within the soil are preparing for growth, much like a baby grows in a womb for many months before emerging into the world. Winter's darkness is a place of necessary quiet to renew strength for the growing season. In spring, the ground begins to thaw and seeds start to rumble as more light and heat reach them. This is the time of the great flowering in the world, followed by a summer of fruitfulness. The hawthorn tree in Ireland is covered with tiny white blossoms in early May and by the end of summer she is laden with haws, her small red fruits. Her leaves and any uneaten fruit falls to the ground to nourish the cycle once again.

This breath prayer helps us to connect to these primal rhythms we see at work in the world around us but that are also guides for our soul's longings. We each have seasons when it is time to blossom and bring fruit to others. But equally so, we each have seasons when we are called to let go of our striving and surrender into the restful arms of winter.

I embrace being,
I release doing.
This day free
from work and worry.

sabbath day

Sabbath is an essential practice in our productivity-oriented, driven, consumeristic culture. To step away from striving and reaching for a day each week is a reminder to us of goodness, of pleasure, of joy as our inheritance.

I consider Sabbath to be the most important contemplative practice I return to and the one that is most challenging. But when I take a break, especially from technology, I experience deep refreshment. It is a wonderful reminder that the world can continue on without me.

In addition to embracing a state of being and letting go of my doing, I try to consciously release thoughts about my work and anxiety in general. For many of us, our work is always accessible, which makes it hard to unplug. For one day a week, I set aside my worries about life and the world as much as possible.

Even if you aren't able to manage a day each week—begin with one hour once a week. Try waking early one day, or one afternoon during your lunch break, turn off your phone and disconnect from technology and breathe. It is more about intention than specific length of time. To create a sanctuary space in the midst of life's urgency and busyness is to claim that there is something deeper and more vital in our lives.

I recommend beginning and ending Sabbath with some kind of simple ritual. Lighting a candle and saying a prayer as you enter the time is a beautiful way to mark that you are entering into sacred time. Spending five minutes breathing and repeating this breath prayer helps to align your intention with the purpose of the Sabbath day.

Breathe in: *I embrace being*,
Breathe out: *I release doing*.
Breathe in: *This day free*
Breathe out: *from work and worry*.

Then, as you move through the day, anytime you find thoughts intruding about what needs to get done, or you feel yourself drawn to check emails, messages, or social media, you can pause for a minute or two to breathe through this prayer.

As you inhale and say *I embrace being*, what do you notice in your body? What sensations arise? As you exhale and say *I release doing*, what images come to mind? Notice any colors that feel connected to this rhythm of embrace and release, or body gestures that might offer an embodied prayer. It could be as simple as crossing your arms around yourself with the inhale and the image of embrace, then letting your arms extend outward with the exhale, your hands and palms open to symbolize release.

For the second half of the breath prayer, I like to rest my hand on my heart as I inhale *This day free* and exhale *from work and worry*. Something about that physical connection to my heart is a reminder of the sanctuary I seek within myself. You might listen for a different gesture that works for you as an expression of this prayer.

How you spend your Sabbath time and what you decide to include and exclude are an important part of the discernment. Without being too rigid, spend some time listening for what activities are most life-giving and which are most life-draining. I love to spend my Sabbath day each week with time for quiet journaling and reflection and a long walk in the woods or by the sea. Time in nature is deeply refreshing and nourishing to me and makes it easier for me to disconnect from my phone and computer than if I spend the day at home.

No matter how busy I am or how much I need to get done, when I make time for Sabbath, I am able to renew myself in ways that won't happen if I just push through. The work I do has more clarity and grace when punctuated by this time of renewal.

In making time for this ancient practice, we affirm again and again the goodness of rest. We celebrate the divine invitation to savor our lives and create spaciousness. We help to create a world that isn't always anxious and obsessed with worry about the future. In saying no for a little while to the busyness, we say yes to what delights and restores us.

I see you with love
gifted, cherished.
Grateful
for who you are.

gazing with love on another

How often do we really see another person as the beautiful gift they are? Perhaps this happens sometimes with those we love, where we are caught in a moment of grace and see them in all their wondrousness and feel full of gratitude for their presence in our lives.

Maybe you have a moment where your eyes meet and you hold each other's gaze for a few breaths as an act of seeing each other with love.

When I work with individuals in spiritual direction and on retreats, I actively try to see them through God's eyes and know how deeply loved they are. I try to bring that loving presence into our time together.

We can intentionally bring this gaze of love to others. You can practice this with a beloved one or a very dear and close friend. You might try setting a timer for one minute and just sit together, eyes softly receiving each other while breathing together and praying quietly in your hearts.

Breathe in: *I see you with love*
Breathe out: *gifted, cherished.*
Breathe in: *Grateful*
Breathe out: *for who you are.*

This can be a very intimate and vulnerable moment because we so rarely spend this kind of time simply looking at another person with love and care.

We can also bring this practice out into the world. How often do we really see another person beneath their role, under our expectations? What if we paused at the grocery store and for a moment brought eyes of love to the stock clerk or the cashier. They don't have to know what you're doing. You don't have to stare, just take in their image, then close your eyes for a moment, breathe, and bathe them with love. Pause and see the other person as beloved and beautiful as they indeed truly are.

We do not want to violate their personal space by holding an uncomfortable gaze, but we can, as the Quaker tradition says, "hold them in the Light," and then pause to hold them with love in our imagination while repeating the breath prayer a few times. To bring a true seeing of others we meet is, in so many traditions, a way of greeting the divine in others, and honoring their dignity and personhood.

This can be such a beautiful way to really start to see people who may have been in some sense "invisible" to us. We can see them as gifts to the world. We can cultivate a deeper kindness within ourselves, too, as we begin to widen our appreciation for others.

I listen for words
that shimmer.
I receive
the invitation.

sacred reading

There are many contemplative ways of being with sacred texts. The ancient practice of *lectio divina*, which means sacred reading, is a way monastics would slow themselves down and listen deeply to sacred texts. They would listen for an invitation that would present itself to their lives, perhaps asking the text, what is calling me, here? The underlying belief is that God speaks to us through words directly to what is happening to us.

One tradition of lectio divina developed by St. Ignatius of Loyola was a way of praying through the Scriptures with all the senses and imagination attuned. This is a creative engagement with the texts, listening for what new voices want to erupt from its midst. This tradition of reading is similar to the Jewish practice of midrash where the words on the page are considered to be black fire and the spaces between are white fire. Midrash seeks to illuminate those spaces between, listening for what is missing, the lost perspectives. We let those gaps in the text and story ask questions, stoke our curiosity, kindle our imagination.

These are many contemplative ways of being with a text and allowing it to transform your heart. Rather than just reading for information and trying to extract information, this kind of reading allows you to be affected by what you read, in intimate relationship with it. The text might be the sacred Scriptures, or a novel or a poem. Whatever text we respectfully enter, this kind of reading asks us to slow way down and rest, knowing that what we read can speak to our heart and to where we are on our journey right now.

As a writer, I find contemplative reading an essential practice for my own creativity. I often will pray *lectio* with a poem as part of my morning prayer and meditation. This allows me to enter into poetic consciousness and shift out of the part of my brain that wants to make plans and get things done. I listen for a line that shimmers for me, a word or phrase that calls to me in some way. I usually feel some kind of energetic response, whether excitement or resistance or curiosity. Sometimes the words have some synchronicity with other events in my life. I trust the shimmering, that it will lead me to the treasure that awaits.

We can practice sacred reading by choosing a text to pray with. It could be from the weekly readings of our faith tradition or a passage that a soul friend recommended we look at. It might be a poem or a section from a book we are reading that has been a soulful companion to us.

Before you begin, pause and quiet your heart. Drop your attention into your body so you are listening from a different part of yourself—this kind of reading isn't about the mind analyzing what we take in. Then take a couple of minutes to simply breathe this prayer before you begin reading. It sets your intention for this time of sacred reading.

Breathe in: *I listen for words*
Breathe out: *that shimmer.*
Breathe in: *I receive*
Breathe out: *the invitation.*

After we read the poem or passage, we let the shimmering phrase unfold within us. Once the sense of invitation arises we can then rest into silence for a few moments, simply resting into being. To close this time, we might repeat the breath prayer again a few times.

This kind of prayer is about opening ourselves to the gifts that await us. It isn't about speed reading for content or instruction. It is about slowing ourselves down enough to hear what shimmers forth, and out of that shimmering what the divine invitation is for us in this moment of our lives. Perhaps a call to a new awareness or action of some kind. It isn't always a new kind of doing; more often it is about a new way of being.

blessing the seasons
of our lives

I breathe in creation's goodness,
I breathe out love.
I am called to my part
in the grand unfolding.

extinction anxiety

The news we receive each day about Earth's suffering and the human impact on it is often overwhelming. It is such a complex and deeply entrenched issue that as individuals we can feel quite helpless. Whether climate change, plastics choking our seas, pollution of air and water, widescale loss of biodiversity and species, or pesticides, there is no shortage of environmental issues to feel deeply concerned and worried about.

There is a growing anxiety over the impact of climate crisis on our daily lives, and our futures, and how slowly some governments and businesses are responding in ways that create change and heal the earth. Within and through that anxiety, there are a few things I seek to remember that help keep me sane and grounded:

1. Mass movements often coalesce quickly and change comes when we least expect it.
2. Spending time regularly savoring Earth—in the garden, a walk in the woods, along a shoreline— helps to center me in ways nothing else can. In honoring the earth in this way, I am also

honoring the ways that so many work to pro-
tect it.

3. I came into this world with a gift I am called
to offer in service. This is my offering; I cannot
do everything.

4. When I allow myself to rest into the unknowing, spend less time planning, more time attun-
ing to the unfolding of things, I feel more
empowered to cooperate with the larger movements at work.

Breath prayer can especially help me with those last
two. I was born with a specific gift to offer the world, my
contribution to healing and restoration. Remembering
this helps me to keep from feeling overwhelmed when I
get stuck in the cycle of anxiety and helplessness and it
seems there is too much to do.

Paired with this prayer of knowing my gift to offer is a
call to rest into the unknowing, to know I don't have to be
the one to figure it all out. Leaning into my breath creates
an inner spaciousness and embodied sense of trust and
ease in what my call is.

Breathe in: *I breathe in creation's goodness,*
Breathe out: *I breathe out love.*
Breathe in: *I am called to my part*
Breathe out: *in the grand unfolding.*

Beginning the breath prayer with a reminder of creation's goodness feels fundamental. It is something I can lean into. I am reminded of the first creation story from Genesis in the Hebrew Scriptures, where after every act of creation God exclaims the goodness of what has just been brought into being. There is a sense of deep delight and enjoyment in all of this creating that we are invited to participate in. When anxiety over environmental degradation sets in, starting from this place of profound reverence for the goodness of the natural world feels fundamental. The breath prayer invites us to this reverence paired with a conscious act of sending love out into the world. To imagine love reaching all the corners of Earth where it is needed.

The second part of the breath prayer is a reminder to us of our individual role in responding, in addition to the reverence and love. We each also have a specific gift that equips us and empowers us to do our part in this crisis, no more and no less. Even if we are uncertain what our particular gift is, breath prayer helps us to slow down, listen, and respond, rather than react or freeze up in anxiety.

When we embrace a posture of humility to the world's woes, we recognize our gifts and limitations. We come to see that we can do something and do it well and release the rest as part of the great collective work.

What you seek
also seeks you.
Rest
and let it find you

discernment

We are each born with a primal orientation toward love and our unique way of bringing it into being in the world. Sometimes we can feel far away from our unique calling, exhausted by life's many and often confusing demands. It can seem like if we were to only work harder, we might come to some deeper understanding of how to direct our life energies. Our Western orientation toward productivity and doing reinforces this sense that if we only try hard enough we will be able to figure out our life direction. If we only earn the right degrees, meet the right people, make enough money, we will feel some satisfaction.

Many years ago, when I finished my PhD studies in theology, I thought I would move into academic teaching as a career. I did work as an adjunct professor for several years but found the administrative side of things quite confining. I was trying to discern what the best way forward was and worked very hard to find the path for me. I created lists of pros and cons. I tried to figure it all out.

Then one day I had a dream where I was scrutinizing a map, and God (who appeared in the form of two koala bears) was ripping the map out of my hands. It was a lovely moment of shifting my perspective and releasing my own plans and maps. That dream and realization were actually the start of a long slow journey of listening. I like to say I am a recovering planner. Not that some plans aren't a good thing, but they aren't a substitute for a deep and reverential listening to the world and our lives.

The clearest moments I have had of discernment have come when I set aside my own needs and desires, tried to release my goals and plans, and really listened for how my life was leading me forward. This listening comes in the form of paying attention to dreams and synchronicities, making art, writing poems, listening attentively to what friends say to me in conversations, and making lots of space for silence. In the stillness I hear a different voice than my own inner planner.

This call we seek also seeks us, and is, in fact, not lost but already inside of us. We just need to listen, to slow ourselves way down, to release our mind's desire to make something happen and simply allow the slow revelation to come to us: to trust the quiet, trust that when we rest we are being deeply nourished for whatever is to come. Trust that what we love and long for also loves and longs for us.

Breathing is also a treasured companion in this process of listening. It is a way of anchoring my awareness in the present moment rather than letting my planning mind run too far into the future. Tending to my breath helps me to stay calmer and more open to insights and intuition. I find the rhythm of breath prayer is much like going for a walk or taking a bath, when the question I had been working on is suddenly working on me.

Breathe in: *What you seek*
Breathe out: *also seeks you.*
Breathe in: *Rest*
Breathe out: *and let it find you*

This breath prayer is for all those times when you find yourself anxiously trying to figure out your life or make something happen. It is for those moments when you see how hard you are working and don't understand why life isn't clearer because of it. It is for when you are relying on the sheer force of your effort and doing.

As you breathe, let your body soften. See if you can let your reaching arms rest by your body, no longer needing to grasp. Notice how your body feels as you invite it into a deep posture of restfulness and openness. These are your only tasks. Breathing, staying open, waiting, noticing.

This prayer can also be especially helpful when combined with images, if that is a way you are drawn to praying. As you breathe in and out—*What you seek also seeks you*—notice what images, colors, or feelings arise. As you continue to breathe—*Rest and let it find you*—again, stay open to any imagery or sensation that accompanies these words and this intention.

As with all of the breath prayers, our intention is to lean deeply into the heart of the sacred Source and find our place of rest there. We can feel ourselves held and sustained during both the ordinary moments and activities of our lives and those fraught with more emotion.

You might practice this breath prayer regularly each morning for ten to twenty minutes during a season of discernment, or you might draw on it in moments when your mind seems to especially want to have things figured out and get a plan together.

Breath prayers are always an invitation into a deep state of rest and presence. When we become attentive to life, life reveals its desires for us.

I breathe in patience
I breathe out grace.
Everything in
the fullness of time

while waiting

Waiting can often feel like a waste of time. How many hours do we spend waiting in traffic, waiting in line at the shop, in the waiting room for the doctor or dentist?

There are many other kinds of waiting as well. Sometimes we wait for news—perhaps whether we got a job we interviewed for or if we were accepted to a program we applied for. Sometimes the waiting is for news of a loved one's health status and whether they are making the journey to recovery. Sometimes we wait for test results that will hopefully indicate why we have been feeling unwell.

Much of our lives are characterized by this waiting in anticipation of something to move, happen, shift, or reveal itself. To rest into the waiting means to yield the part of ourselves that wants to get somewhere, get something done, or know the answer. Waiting invites us to the practice of patience.

In the desert tradition, the Greek term for patience is *hupomone*. The desert way of patience means to sit still and stay with yourself. The temptation is to distract ourselves, to avoid discomfort, to feel we have some form of control over our lives. Today we have all kinds of distractions, technology and our mobile gadgets the most immediately available ones. But there have always been ways to distract ourselves while waiting for something else.

This was what the monk's cell symbolized in the desert tradition; it was the place of radical encounter with oneself and ultimately the divine presence. The cell requires patience, which means growing more at ease with time's often slow passage and opening to an encounter with the divine there.

Theologian David Keller in his book *Oasis of Wisdom* writes:

Time was experienced differently by the desert elders. Chronological time depends on duration. It can impose limitations on the ego when it is associated with completing a goal. It establishes a boundary for expectations and the ego strains to accomplish what it desires. Time accentuates the need for control of what happens within time. This is a major source of anxiety and despair.

He goes on to point out that patience enters in as the resistance to the sense of "affliction, waiting, anxiety" that comes with duration, and it is in this resistance that the soul is fashioned.

You might begin this breath practice the next time you are stopped at a traffic signal or in a long line at the grocery store. Notice those times you feel especially impatient or ready to move to the next thing. What happens when you pause and soften and allow yourself to dwell in this moment? Can waiting become its own kind of meditation?

Breathe in: *I breathe in patience*
Breathe out: *I breathe out grace*
Breathe in: *Everything in*
Breathe out: *the fullness of time*

Let your breath become an anchor for your awareness in this moment, so you are no longer in anticipation of what comes next but simply as present as you can be. Your breath can become a way into this moment now.

As you breathe in, invite in the quality of patience. Notice any images that accompany this word for you. What does patience look like or feel like?

As you breathe out, consciously send the quality of grace out into the world. Grace is a kind of mercy we do not need to earn. It is freely given in abundance and we can experience it ourselves and wish it for others. Ask yourself, what does grace feel like or look like as I breathe?

The second breath is a reminder that *Everything in the fullness of time*. This is a statement as much as it is an

187

invitation to live into its truth. We do not control time, as much as we might try with our multitasking and efficiency plans. Time unfolds in its own rhythm. Sometimes it feels regimented and fleeting, the *chronos* time of our days. Sometimes it feels generous and eternal, the *kairos* time of moments when we slip beneath the surface of our obsession with tasks and allow ourselves to fall in love with the here and now.

Crossing over
the veil is thin.

crossing a doorway or threshold

In Ireland you sometimes find a Brigid's cross hanging over a doorway as a blessing of protection. When you enter a Catholic church, there is usually a holy water font inside the door with the invitation to bless yourself. In Jewish tradition the *mezuzah* hangs by the door as a sign of blessing. What might be your own threshold crossing ritual? Even just pausing to touch the doorposts with your hands and let your feet linger on the threshold while breathing and offering the breath prayer above is a simple yet powerful ritual of remembering.

Doorways are not just practical means of leaving or entering. They evoke the transition points within us and invite questions about what inner landscapes we are departing from or arriving to.

The root of the word *threshold* is connected to the act of "threshing." The work of threshing is one of separating the edible grains and seeds from the outer husks and chaff. The origin of the word *thresh* evokes a sense of turning and returning. Thresholds are not only exterior, like a doorway or gate, but also interior, in places where something is ending and something is beginning. When we cross a doorway, whether into or out of our homes, or into a sacred space like a church or temple, we are also invited to consider doorways in our own lives.

You might practice opening and closing doors with care. Sometimes a door we want to pass through is locked and we have to knock or ring to gain entry. Some doors are always open and some are sealed shut. So it is within ourselves as well.

If we are paying attention, we might discover just how many doorways we cross in any given day. Leaving home, arriving to work, going into a bathroom, kitchen, or closet. The door of our car or public transit. The door of the market or bank.

This breath prayer can be whispered as you are approaching the doorway and crossing it. It is a reminder of the Celtic belief that at thresholds the veil between worlds is especially thin, meaning that heaven and earth feel closer together. Every time we cross a doorway, we have an opportunity to remember this truth.

The Celtic spirituality of the ancients had an expansive definition of thresholds; they could be seasonal turnings like the solstices and equinoxes, turning from dawn to dusk, sacred places like a grove of trees or a holy well, as well as experiences like going on a pilgrimage. Doorways offer the most physical and tangible reminder of these crossing-over points.

Breathe in: *Crossing over*
Breathe out: *the veil is thin.*

As you breathe in, depending on whether you are leaving or arriving via the doorway, you can say *crossing over* as you physically move across the threshold. Then with the exhale, say *the veil is thin* as a way of honoring the sacredness of this experience and its possibility and potential for revealing what is behind the veil, if only for a moment. Become aware of the sacred presence here. What does the God of thresholds invite us to consider?

One of the things I love most about living in Europe is all the beautiful old doorways, especially those at the entrance to churches and cathedrals. Often ornate with large hinges and carved figures and designs, they spark a longing in my heart to name the threshold within me.

But even the very simple wood doors in my own home, mass produced and nondescript, provide me both with thresholds out into the world as well as a way of crossing back into my sanctuary space. The doors within our home remind me of the gift of having many rooms to work and rest in. They remind me of all my inner rooms I have yet to explore.

Praise the rain
quenching Earth's thirst.
Let greening flourish
in and around me.

for a rainy day

Since 2003 I have lived in places where it rains a lot. First in Seattle, Washington—the Emerald City—and then in Galway, Ireland—the Emerald Isle. What keeps these places so green as to earn the title "emerald" is, of course, the abundance of rainfall. It was while living in the Pacific Northwest that I discovered the saying about moss growing on the north side didn't actually apply there. Moss grows on all sides in the Northwest, and in Ireland, too, where rain and damp dominate, especially in the winter season.

It was in Seattle where I learned to love the rain. I soon discovered my inner hermit loved long quiet afternoons reading or journaling or simply listening to the rain patter on the windows. Even going for a walk could be a special treat because the streets were so much quieter with everyone else staying in and trying to stay dry. In Ireland, my husband and I joke that the rain takes itself even more seriously here (than Seattle). Here, there are all kinds of words for it: mizzling, lashing, and bucketing.

St. Hildegard of Bingen, a twelfth-century German mystic, coined the term *viriditas*, which essentially means the greening power of God. The Rhine valley where she lived is another lush and fertile place, and she saw the greenness of the world around her as a sign of its fecundity and life-giving power.

This greening isn't just an external sign of nourishment and vitality, it also points to our internal state as well. Hildegard would look at both body and soul through this lens of greening. She would ask: Where is the flow of *viriditas* blocked and how could one encourage its movement again? In the body, this often manifests as illness, while in the soul it can manifest as spiritual dryness or aridity. We all experience times and seasons when we feel keenly the waning of our enthusiasm for life or prayer. We can give thanks for the rains that come to quench the thirst of the land and in our hearts.

This breath prayer is one to practice on a day when it is raining outside. Maybe you have the gift of staying indoors, cuddled with a book, gazing out the window. Or maybe you have to go to work and the rain is slowing down traffic or making your bus commute more difficult. Maybe you have to walk somewhere in the rain.

However you feel about the rain, this prayer invites you into a sense of gratitude for its greening gifts. To practice, pause while the rain is falling and listen for a few moments just to the sound of it. If you are outside, turn

196

your face upward and feel it washing your face. Breathe in and out a few times simply to inhale the scent of rain falling. There is even a word for the smell of rain falling on dry soil, *petrichor*.

After feeling this sense-connection to the rain, you can then repeat this breath prayer to further deepen your encounter and appreciation of this gift.

Breathe in: *Praise the rain*
Breathe out: *quenching Earth's thirst.*
Breathe in: *Let greening flourish*
Breathe out: *in and around me.*

As you breathe in and out, you might imagine the color green infusing you with the in-breath and blessing the world with the out-breath.

As you breathe in and say *Praise the rain*, see if you can really call upon that sense of gratitude for the gift that rain offers. As you breathe out and say *quenching Earth's thirst*, remember a time when you were so thirsty and were able to finally get a large glass of water. Several years ago while on retreat in Austria in August, after a long hike on a very hot day, I found a gushing spring with ice cold water. Plunging my hands and face in were so delicious I still remember the moment clearly.

As you breathe in and say *Let greening flourish*, imagine you are blessing yourself and the world with this gift of vital greenness. As you breathe out and say *in and around me*, see that greening power fill you and fill the world.

Praise the sun's
warm glow.
Illuminating the world,
calling forth my light.

for a sunny day

While the earth needs rain for growth, it also needs sunlight in equal measure. One of my favorite experiences living in Ireland is the time that follows a heavy rainfall, when the clouds break apart and sunlight shimmers off wet surfaces and dazzles the world. Something about the pewter of clouds and the gold gleam of the sun creates a moment that is always magical. Rainbows often follow.

Or those abundant summer months when the longer warmer days allow the herbs on my terrace to flourish and bloom, and the farmer's markets are piled high with berries, stone fruits, lettuces, and sweet tomatoes. When the days are warm and sunny, I can swim in the sea or walk in the forest, where I see the light filtered by leaves.

How many of us want to bask on a warm sunny afternoon when we have nothing to do but linger in the warm air until the late sunset? Closing our eyes with face upturned to that brilliant yellow orb, swimming outside, feeling breezes on bare skin. We may touch the carefree moments of childhood on summer vacation with nothing but time to play.

We can pause in these moments to give thanks for sunlight—whether a winter storm giving way to brilliant reflections on wet ground or a perfect summer day when we feel like we could linger forever.

On a day when the sun is shining, even if only for a brief while, you can pause and close your eyes. Press your face toward the sun and her warm light. Notice the color inside your eyelids, feel the warmth of her radiance on your skin. Imagine gold light dancing within you and all around you.

Then breathe slowly for a few moments, simply taking in the experience of sunlight. Feel the gratitude spread through your whole being. Imagine being like a plant that is feeling the sun on its green leaves for the first time in a long while, taking in that gift.

Then enter into the breath prayer.

Breathe in: *Praise the sun's*
Breathe out: *warm glow.*
Breathe in: *Illuminating the world,*
Breathe out: *calling forth my light.*

As you breathe in saying *Praise the sun's*, feel the gratitude rise up in you. Let your heart expand to welcome in this gift. As you breathe out and say *warm glow*, feel the golden glow spread through your whole body starting in your heart center.

Breathing in again, say *Illuminating the world* and imagine every corner of Earth painted with this golden light. Breathing out, say *calling forth my light*, and rest for a moment and open to how the light in you wants to join the light already illuminating the world.

Imagine the way sunlight helps to call forth the greening of plant life, imagine the sun is also calling forth the renewal of life within you. What is the light you bring into the world?

Light has been a powerful metaphor in mystical tradition for the ways that God illumines the world and our hearts. In the story of St. Benedict, it is said that toward the end of his life, he received a vision: In the middle of the night, he suddenly beheld a flood of light shining down from above, more brilliant than the sun, and with it every trace of darkness cleared away. According to his own description, the whole world was gathered up before his eyes "in what appeared to be a single ray of light."

In the concluding meditation he created for the Spiritual Exercises, St. Ignatius invites the reader into a Contemplation on the Love of God. After reflecting on God's gifts and work in the world, we are invited to consider the limitless quality of God's love, imagining them as rays from the sun. Let this breath prayer open your heart in gratitude for all the gifts the sun brings to the world.

Night falls and stars glimmer,
I behold the universe.

gazing at the stars

I live in a city, so light pollution from streetlamps at night means the stars are not as vivid as they might be further out in the country. But even so, at night or early morning, especially in winter when the dark hours are more extended, I take my dog out to relieve herself and am sometimes stopped short by a clear sky overhead and a vision of such expansiveness. Because I live in Ireland, the sky is often cloudy or rainy, so times when it is clear are extra special.

I am grateful for these moments, which pull me out of the comfort of home, and I can stand for a few moments, under the wide darkness, taking in thousands of points of light circling overhead, tracking the moon in her phases. These are heart-expanding moments when I feel my smallness in the universe, but it is freeing. I can lean into cycles which aren't measured in days, weeks, months, or years, but epochs and aeons. I can touch eternity.

Try making it a practice to step outside each night before going to sleep for five minutes. Let your eyes adjust to the darkness and gaze upward at the sky. Let your eyes slowly scan across the heavens.

Breathe in: *Night falls and stars glimmer*,
Breathe out: *I behold the universe*.

This breath prayer invites you into a stance of wonder. This might be one of the prayers that especially calls or one of the divine names to be breathed in and out. Maybe add a breath in saying *God* and a breath out saying *of mystery* followed by the breath prayer above. Consider what names of God are inspired by this vision.

Imagine your ancestors standing under this same sky and what it might have whispered to them. Many used to navigate by celestial bodies. Most living in the United States have ancestors from elsewhere who likely travelled by ship to arrive, while following the sky's guidance. Following the North Star is a metaphor for following the trail to our purpose or life meaning. Of course, the magi are said to have followed the star to find the infant Jesus.

Chet Raymo, a naturalist and professor of physics, wrote many books about developing a more intimate connection to the universe with the qualities of reverence, awe, gratitude, and praise. In his book *An Intimate Look at the Night Sky*, he writes,

> Let the children know. Let them know that nothing, nothing they'll find in the virtual world of e-games, television, or the Internet matters half as

much as a glitter of stars on an inky sky, drawing our attention into the incomprehensible mystery of why the universe is here at all, and why we are here to observe it. The winter Milky Way rises in the east, one trillion individually invisible points of light, one trillion revelations of the Ultimate Mystery, conferring on the watcher a dignity, a blessedness, that confounds the dull humdrum of the commonplace and opens a window to infinity.

Whether or not we have young children, we can draw ourselves away from our gadgets and electronic devices for a span of time and allow the great swath of stars to evoke wonder and delight in us. It is almost impossible to stand for a while under the night sky and not be moved to wonder at the great mystery of things. To feel our smallness in the midst of such expanse.

Much in the way these breath prayers try to break us open to the power of presence to ordinary moments, gazing at the stars reminds us that the world is so much bigger than our limited selves.

There is a beautiful gift of humility that comes when we realize we are not the center of things. With all that we must deal with as human beings, there is a vast universe surrounding us with untold possibilities.

I see the radiance
each moment reveals.
It plants seeds of joy
in my heart.

encountering beauty

When you encounter beauty in the world, you drop out of goal-consciousness and into witness-consciousness. Instead of being driven by the mindset of productivity, you shift into a mindset of beholding the moment. To behold is to stand with openness and awe before what is happening, rather than trying to figure out what to do next. To see beauty and truly receive it means to be caught in a moment of savoring. We temporarily let go of our perpetual self-improvement projects, life goals, productivity charts, and to-do lists.

The more we give ourselves over to beauty, or moments that are radiant through their ordinary appearance, the more we might start to see that these are what a meaningful life is built upon. The more I give myself over to these encounters with radiance, the more I find my purpose in this simple act of being present to the beauty in the ordinary. What if our purpose here is to behold, to witness, to reverence, to cherish the beauty that erupts all around us?

Dr. Alejandro Garcia-Rivera, a professor of mine in graduate school, said that "beauty is that which moves the human heart." Beauty breaks open the most ordinary moments, shattering the illusion of ordinariness and banality. Whether the way sunlight streams in to illuminate the fruit sitting on our kitchen counter or how birdsong erupts through our window each morning, or how an act of kindness from a loved one can make us feel seen and heard in the midst of a difficult day. These are all forms of beauty. It might be an encounter with nature—seeing the true brilliance of a flower, a photograph posted to social media that captures a moment with such vision, or perhaps a simple moment of generosity—anything that causes you to catch your breath, to pause, to gaze and look more closely.

In these moments, we are invited to pause and savor. The root of the word savor is *saporem* in Latin, which is related to *sapientiae*, the word for wisdom. To slow down and savor is to cultivate wisdom in our lives.

When a moment arrests your attention, before moving on to the next thing, take some time to pause. This breath prayer is one way to honor your experience and feel its fullness.

Breathe in: *I see the radiance*
Breathe out: *each moment reveals.*
Breathe in: *It plants seeds of joy*
Breathe out: *in my heart.*

The first part of the breath prayer is an acknowledgment of what you are seeing, whatever specific form it takes. The second part of the prayer is an honoring of how it impacts you in an ongoing way. Giving ourselves over to beauty means making more room for delight, wonder, awe, joyfulness. We can cultivate a sense of interior expansiveness by cherishing all the ways beauty is made manifest around us.

The river of grief
no way but through.

in the midst of loss

Wwhen my mother died suddenly in 2003, I descended into a deep river of grief for a long time. We were very close and despite her having been chronically ill for many years, her death came as a very unwelcome surprise. My husband John and I had just moved to Seattle, Washington, from the Bay Area in California. We had new jobs, a new home, a new community, and had left our close friends behind, so while there was much excitement, it was a lonely season.

I was only thirty-three years old and had just finished graduate school. Those days, weeks, and months that followed her loss are hard to remember. I developed fatigue and headaches and other physical ailments as manifestations of my grief. Living in a culture that doesn't honor grief's timeline, I found most people stopped asking how I was doing within a month following my loss. One of my new friends was a rabbi who had also lost both her parents. She told me in Jewish tradition when you lose someone close to you, you go into a special status for a year where nothing extra is expected of you because of the work grief demands. Her words gave me permission to stop trying to push so much.

I was also lucky during that time to find a Jungian analyst who helped me navigate that dark terrain and show up for my grief as fully as possible. He encouraged me to see the only way through grief was to welcome it, immerse myself in it, let it flow through me. He helped me to see that making space for the full experience of grief was necessary for healing.

During that time, there were many lines from sacred texts that called to me, including in the story of Rachel's loss of her children: "A voice is heard in Ramah, lamentation and bitter weeping. Rachel is weeping for her children; she refuses to be comforted for her children, for they are no more." This idea that she refused to be consoled was in its own way comforting to me, to know someone else who experienced the depths of grief as well and refused society's pressure to move on.

Another passage that became a close companion was Psalm 56:8. "You have collected all my tears in your bottle." I was consoled by the idea that God was so intimate with me in my grief that my tears were counted and gathered. I kept imagining how enormous this bottle would have to be.

Either of those Scripture verses could make a potent breath prayer for loss and grief. I settled on the one below because the image of traveling grief's river of tears became an important one for me. When we experience profound loss, there is no shortcut to experiencing and honoring the grief we feel. Often, the only thing I found I could do was to lean into my breath as an anchor to keep me from drowning.

Breathe in: *The river of grief*
Breathe out: *no way but through.*

Breathing in, imagine grief as a river flowing. There is no way to stop it, no use in trying to push against it. Breathing out, see it flowing through you. Soften any resistance you might have. Allow the river to bring tears and sorrow, welcome it in as much as possible. When tears arise, many of us try to shut them down. When we allow the tears to come, they help us to express the deep grief we are carrying. They can help us with the slow journey of healing. If tears don't come, try just making a space of possibility for their arrival. Nothing needs to be forced here; we follow the river and whatever it brings.

The breath is a tremendous ally when we are going through something challenging. Think of the ways that women who are giving birth draw on their breath to help them move through the pain they are experiencing. Following the inhale and exhale allows us to endure more

215

than we think we are capable of. The simple act of slowing and deepening our breath helps regulate our nervous system and calm us. Connecting the breath to an image helps us to imagine our way through.

One thing I found profoundly helpful in those days of grief's freshness, especially as I tried to navigate a new life and job teaching at university, was to set aside time each day to be with my sorrow. I found that rather than try to resist feeling my grief—and then having it erupt in moments I wasn't expecting—I could create a daily ritual of being present to my feelings of loss. I could allow a half hour or hour to simply show up for myself and whatever wanted to come through. I would breathe and pray with this image of letting grief's river flow over and through me. I would remember my mother and feel the terrible ache of her loss. I would let my own tears flow. This helped to create a sacred container for my journey, while also allowing me to function in my daily life. Tears would still come in moments I didn't expect them or even welcome them, but I had a way to honor the reality of what I was going through.

Now I am revealing
new things to you.

learning something new

Soon after John and I moved to Galway in Ireland, we decided to take an Irish language class together. I was fascinated by all the ancient place names that appear on signs in both Irish and English. The original Irish names tell the story of a place through the words used. The English names, however, are just a transliteration, trying to simply keep the pronunciation from the Irish, and the places lose their meaning to those who don't understand the original language. Having learned French and German as a child and always doing well with language, I thought this would come naturally. Instead, I found myself week after week struggling to have my mouth make the same sounds our teacher would make. The pronunciation, along with spelling rules, pushed me to my edges. I discovered that there is a great gift in trying to learn something new, in putting myself in such a vulnerable spot, and in remembering what it is like to feel like you don't know anything. It was humbling to see how bad I was at this.

When we meet challenges or step into something we hope will challenge us—in studies, in work, in creative directions for our lives—we often value the experience.

Learning offers us the opportunities for growth and humility in the process. We might see all the ways we defend ourselves from being vulnerable or appearing like we don't know anything. It is in allowing ourselves to be humbled that we often break open to new things. In monastic tradition the practice of conversion is the lifetime commitment to always being a beginner and always beginning again.

One of my favorite Scripture verses is from the prophet Isaiah:

> Now I am revealing new things to you, things hidden and unknown to you, created just now, this very moment, of these things you have heard nothing until now, so that you cannot say, "Oh yes, I knew this."

That first line in particular is very hopeful and speaks to beginnings. I breathe in and say *now I am revealing*, I breathe out and say *new things to you*. This prayer invites me into a deep trust that there are actions or unfoldings at work beneath the surface. Learning something new isn't just about feeling awkward and imperfect but also about creating new habits, rhythms, and skills for our lives.

* * *

Perhaps practicing these breath prayers has been a new learning experience for you. At the start it may have felt awkward or unnatural to pray in this way. But slowly, over time, with commitment and diligence, perhaps you discovered a new ally in the spiritual life. Your breath may now be a dear and treasured companion, and these prayers may have become words of commitment to seeking the sacred in every moment.

My hope is that you have found even one breath prayer that has become a source of consolation in your life. Just as with everything new that we learn, there is a period of stretching and growing that can be uncomfortable at times. If we commit to working through that stretching until we find our soul's capacity has widened, we discover a new breadth to our experience. We can cultivate a deeper presence to the joys and sorrows of life, breathing through and with them, and in the process show up in the world more fully as ourselves.

composing your own breath prayers

Hopefully this book has served as a doorway for you to deeper attentiveness into ordinary moments. In the introduction I talked about how these breath prayers are about cultivating greater presence, stability, and gratitude for the moments of our lives.

Perhaps you worked your way through each breath prayer methodically, trying each one out, repeating them until you had learned them by heart. Or maybe you looked through the topics and selected two or three that called to you and focused on those.

I tried to cover a wide range of daily moments and tasks from the very mundane to the more seasonal. Maybe you have a daily task I missed and you'd love to create your own breath prayer to bring your attention more fully to it. Or perhaps you wanted to put different words to an activity I covered here. I invite you into your own compositions and creations.

There are two main ways you might approach this.

The first is to call the activity to mind and heart and listen for the prayer you want to offer while engaging in it. This might be a simple prayer for becoming more present to the moment, or it might be a prayer for how this activity has the potential to transform you and your awareness. Both are wonderful approaches. The activity has value in itself and each moment is a doorway to transformation, to seeing life in a new way. You can experiment with the words and then link them to your inhale and exhale. Then practice your new breath prayer whenever you can, resting into the words you created to support you. You might also engage in this activity and ask the Divine to inspire you with the right words, asking for help and support in creating the prayer that will be nourishing.

The other way to do this is to keep alert to lines from Scripture or poems that inspire you. Sometimes a phrase arrives to us in a way that it feels like a gift. You can then draw on this phrase to create a breath prayer and consider which activity it might be in support of.

Years ago, for example, I fell in love with David Whyte's poem "What to Remember When Waking," and the line "what you can plan is too small for you to live" felt luminous for me as a recovering planner. Soon it became a mantra for me. I found myself often breathing it in, *what I can plan*, then breathing out, *is too small for me*, adapting the words slightly for my prayer. I often prayed this prayer when I found myself trying to figure things out too much, trying to control how things unfolded.

Or Jane Hirshfield's poem "Lake and Maple," where I first encountered this line during a period of great grief: "The still heart that refuses nothing." I found myself praying it in moments when I wanted to push everything away. It invited me to rest into the stillness of my heart and create a welcoming space for whatever was arising moment by moment. Breathing in, I pray *the still heart*, breathing out, I whisper *that refuses nothing*. I see the deep stillness within me and I let go of any resistance I have as much as possible.

I am also thinking of poems like Pablo Neruda's series of odes to ordinary activities. In his "Ode to Ironing," he has many beautiful lines, but I might take "the holy surfaces are smoothed out" and create my own breath prayer for ironing from it. I breathe in *the holy surfaces* and breathe out *are smoothed out*. As I pass the iron over the fabric, I can experience that smoothing in a concrete way. I can see my clothing as holy surfaces, worthy of blessing.

Another one of my favorite Scripture passages is from the prophet Jeremiah:

Thus says the Lord:
Stand at the crossroads, and look,
   and ask for the ancient paths,
where the good way lies; and walk in it,
   and find rest for your souls.

Sometimes when I go on pilgrimage I adapt this prayer for myself.

Breathe in: *Stand at the crossroads*,
Breathe out: *ask for ancient paths*.

Breathe in: *Walk in it*
Breathe out: *find rest for my soul.*

Each moment of breath helps me to deepen into the invitation of this passage. I start with standing at the crossroads, really feeling myself on a threshold. I then ask for the ancient paths and my heart lifts to the divine, asking for wisdom and guidance. I then walk in it, which means to practice and commit to this way, and finally, I find rest for my soul. With that final exhale, my body feels a deep release.

As you create or discover your own breath prayers, consider what activities during your day you would love to bless with more awareness and presence. Also consider the phrases and lines from sacred texts that already inspire you and how they might help you to breathe more deeply into your life right now.

But also open to your own words, the prayers of your heart that rise up and want to honor particular activities that feel integral to your day. Let those words bless and reveal the way the sacred is already present to you.

Notes

Epigraph

v **"A new moon teaches gradualness"**: Rumi, *The Essential Rumi*, trans. Coleman Barks (New York: HarperCollins, 1995), 151.

Introduction

2 **"The Divine has sent us a Comforter"**: AKL, "Comforter," Uradiance, 2021, https://tinyurl.com/3jzwsf6v (used with permission).

3 **"St. Paul's invitation to people who hold faith to 'pray without ceasing.'"**: 1 Thessalonians 5:17.

6 **"St. Hesychios the Priest writes"**: St. Hesychios the Priest, I, "On Watchfulness and Holiness," in *Philokalia—The Eastern Christian Spiritual Texts* (SkyLight Illuminations), trans. G. E. H. Palmer, Philip Sherrard, and BishopKalistos Ware (Nashville, TN: Turner, 2006), sec. 100, Kindle.

14 **"'I was on watch and God came to me'"**: (John the Dwarf 27).

15 **"The Indian Poet Kabir wrote"**: Daniel Ladinsky, *Love Poems from God: Twelve Sacred Voices from the East and West* (New York: Penguin, 2002), 227.

Entering the Practice

45 **"'Listen, are you breathing just a little and calling it a life?'"**: Mary Oliver, "Have You Ever Tried to Enter the Long Black Branches," from *West Wind: Poems and Prose Poems* (Boston: Mariner, 1998).

The Grace of Daily Tasks

68 **"one where we look with the 'eyes of your heart,'"**: Ephesians 1:18.

75 **"God 'walks among the pots and pans'"**: Marc Foley, *St. Teresa of Avila: The Book of Her Foundations* (Washington, DC: ICS, 2011), 67.

76 **"Buddhist monk Thich Nhat Hanh writes"**: Thich Nhat Hanh, *The Sun My Heart: From Mindfulness to Insight Contemplation* (London: Random House, 1992), 17.

81 **"'then pinning it to the line with two wooden clothespins'"**: Barbara Brown Taylor, *An Altar in the World* (New York: HarperCollins, 2009), 46.

97 **"Wendell Berry gives advice to 'stay away from screens'"**: Wendell Berry, *New Collected Poems* (Berkeley, CA: Counterpoint, 2012), 354.

104 **"In these moments, the wisdom of Buddhist teacher Thich Nhat Hanh reminds me"**: Thich Nhat Hanh, *The Miracle of Mindfulness: An Introduction to the Practice of Meditation* (Boston: Beacon, 1999).

108 **"'the breathing together of all things'"**: Esther de Waal, *The Celtic Way of Prayer* (New York: Doubleday, 1997), xv.

Sanctifying Time

125 **"'Let its weight fall back into the earth'"**: Rilke, *In Praise of Mortality—Selections from Rainer Maria Rilke's "Duino Elegies and Sonnets to Orpheus."* Translated and edited by Anita Barrows and Joanna Macy (New York: Riverhead, 2005).

129 **"'The night will give you a horizon / further than you can see'"**: David Whyte, *Essentials* (Langley, WA: Many Rivers Press, 2020), Kindle.

132 **"It makes me part of possibility. It gives me hope"**: Joan Chittister, *In the Heart of the Temple* (New York: BlueBridge, 2004).

138 **"Beginning requires that I remain willing to act, and to summon my hopes in the face of torpor"**: Kathleen Norris, *Acedia and Me* (New York: Riverhead Books, 2010), 185.

145 **"'Now is the time to know that all you do is sacred'"**: Hafiz, "Today," from *The Gift: Poems of Hafiz*, trans. Daniel Ladinsky (New York: Penguin, 1999).

149 **"'Perhaps the truth depends on a walk around a lake'"**: Wallace Stevens, *The Collected Poems* (New York: Vintage, 2015), 408.

Blessing the Seasons of Our Lives

186 **"'This is a major source of anxiety and despair"**: Christine Valters Paintner, *Desert Fathers and Mothers* (Woodstock, VT: SkyLight Paths, 2012), 102.

203 **"'in what appeared to be a single ray of light'"**: Saint Gregory the Great, *Dialogues on the Miracles of the Italian Fathers*, vol. 39 (Washington, DC: Ex Fontibus, 2016), 201.

207 **"a blessedness, that confounds the dull humdrum of the commonplace and opens a window to infinity":** Chet Raymo, *An Intimate Look at the Night Sky* (New York: Walker, 2001), 215.

214 **"'she refuses to be comforted for her children, for they are no more":** Jeremiah 31:15.

214 **"You have collected all my tears in your bottle":** New Living Translation (NLT).

220 **"so that you cannot say, 'Oh yes, I knew this'":** Isaiah 48:6–7, Jerusalem Bible translation.

Composing Your Own Breath Prayers

226 **"'what you can plan is too small for you to live'":** David Whyte, *River Flow: New and Selected Poems* (Langley, WA: Many Rivers Press, 2007).

226 **"'The still heart that refuses nothing'":** Jane Hirshfield, "Lake and Maple," in *Lives of the Heart: Poems* (New York: Harper Perennial, 1997).

227 **"but I might take 'the holy surfaces are smoothed out'":** Pablo Neruda, *Full Woman, Fleshly Apple, Hot Moon: Selected Poems of Pablo Neruda*, trans. Stephen Mitchell (New York: HarperCollins, 1997), 235.

227 **"and find rest for your souls":** Jeremiah 6:16.